FAMILY LAW ADVOCACY

The role of the law in settling family disputes has been a matter of particular debate over the past 25 years. In keeping with the general public perception, the media have been largely critical about the role of lawyers in family law matters, sustaining a general lack of confidence in the legal profession, and a more specific feeling that in family matters lawyers aggravate conflict or even represent a female conspiracy. The climate in which family lawyers practise in England and Wales is therefore a harsh one.

The authors of this path-breaking study felt it was time to find out more about the contribution of barristers in family law cases. They therefore embarked on a careful study of the family law bar, its characteristics, what its members do and how their activities contribute to the management or resolution of family disputes. Much of the study comprises an in-depth examination of the day-to-day activity of members of the family law bar through observation of individual barristers as they perform their role in the context of a court hearing,

In attempting to answer questions such as whether our family justice system is excessively adversarial, or whether family barristers earn too much from human unhappiness or indeed whether those working in the front line of child protection earn enough, the authors reach some surprising conclusions. 'The barrister is both mentor and guide for the client' is how they begin their conclusion; 'we hope that we have shown that society should value their contribution more' is how they finish.

Family Law Advocacy

How Barristers help the Victims of Family Failure

Mavis Maclean

and

John Eekelaar

·HART·
PUBLISHING

OXFORD AND PORTLAND, OREGON
2009

Published in North America (US and Canada) by
Hart Publishing
c/o International Specialized Book Services
920 NE 58th Avenue, Suite 300
Portland, OR 97213–3786
USA
Tel: +1 503 287 3093 or toll-free: (1) 800 944 6190
Fax: +1 503 280 8832
E-mail: orders@isbs.com
Website: http://www.isbs.com

Hart Publishing Ltd, 16C Worcester Place, Oxford, OX1 2JW
Telephone: +44 (0)1865 517530 Fax: +44 (0)1865 510710
E-mail: mail@hartpub.co.uk
Website: http://www.hartpub.co.uk

British Library Cataloguing in Publication Data
Data Available

ISBN: 978-1-84113-277-8

Typeset by Columns Design Ltd, Reading
Printed and bound in Great Britain by
TJ International Ltd, Padstow, Cornwall

Table of Contents

Table of Contents

1

Preconceptions

I. Introduction

OUR BOOK *Family Lawyers* was subtitled, *The Divorce Work of Solicitors*.[1] The subtitle demonstrated that we were examining only part of what family lawyers do. It did not cover any family law work done by the other branch of the legal profession, the barristers. Barristers, to be sure, did occasionally appear in the book in what could have been seen as cameo roles. They are referred to as being used in order to persuade clients to take a more realistic view of their case, and so speed things up;[2] or as factors leading to increased costs,[3] and one was reported as suggesting the questionable tactic of implying that a wife could not find employment by 'binning' job offers or invitations for interview.[4] Clearly our account of the implementation of family law was incomplete without an examination of the part played by barristers.

There is little research published about barristers' work. Adam Kramer has recently written a 'guide to becoming a barrister in England and Wales',[5] which provides a useful description of the many types of work undertaken by barristers, the steps necessary towards qualification and, interestingly from our perspective, short accounts by young barristers of their day-to-day activities over a week. This includes an account by a 'white female' in her fifth year of chambers' tenancy of her work in

---

[1] J Eekelaar, M Maclean and S Beinart, *Family Lawyers: The Divorce Work of Solicitors* (Oxford, Hart Publishing, 2000).

[2] *Ibid*, at 172.

[3] *Ibid*, at 174, 177, 178.

[4] *Ibid*, at 118.

[5] A Kramer, *Bewigged and Bewildered?* (Oxford, Hart Publishing, 2007).

family and prison law,[6] which will have a strong resonance with the descriptions we offer in this book. However the book makes no claim to be an account of research.

John Morison and Philip Leith's account of 'the barrister's world', published over 15 years ago,[7] is, however, a substantial research study. The study was based on interviews with barristers, though unfortunately it is not revealed how the barristers were selected, or indeed the number who were interviewed. However, it did seem to include barristers of different levels of experience, in both civil and criminal law practices. The main thrust of the findings was that barristers regarded themselves as 'persuaders'—whether of the parties they were representing, the opposing parties, or the courts—rather than as legal oracles, seeking out legal truths and applying them to facts. This led the authors to question whether academic writers of textbooks which attempted to articulate 'correct' legal propositions represented the 'reality' of law.[8] Rather, they concluded that 'legal knowledge' was a 'process', constituted by 'a host of conflicting beliefs and practices' which were 'strategic and negotiable rather than fixed and static'.[9] Whether it is helpful to represent the way lawyers grind out their perceptions of the law and the facts in concrete cases as a 'more real' version of the law than analysis of legal propositions could be debated. The fact that people do *argue* about the correctness of legal propositions demonstrates that there is a kind of reality which can be comprehended in this discourse, even though it might be one which is constructed by the protagonists themselves.[10] One might say the same of aesthetic principles, except that for law the propositions can in certain circumstances affect practical decision-making, and thereby affect people's lives, whereas an aesthetic theory may only affect the nature of a work of art or its performance.[11]

---

[6] Kramer, *ibid*, at 54–61.

[7] J Morison and P Leith, *The Barrister's World and the Nature of Law* (Milton Keynes, Open University, 1992).

[8] *Ibid*, at 182.

[9] *Ibid*, at 195.

[10] This point has been strongly associated with R Dworkin: see *Law's Empire* (London, Fontana Press, 1986) ch 1.

[11] Nor does it seem right to conclude that their evidence of the way barristers work refutes positivism, and particularly the work of Herbert Hart, which is strangely dismissed as 'middle-class' (at 174), as if the theory could not have been propounded by or perhaps be comprehended by a member of the aristocracy or the working class. But there is ample space within Hart's exposition of the 'open texture' of law and the role of prediction to embrace the practices of barristers as explained by Morison and Leith, and Joseph Raz's later insistence of the necessity for judicial decision to provide authoritative determinations of law seems quite untouched by it.

But whatever view one takes of Morison and Leith's conclusions about the 'nature' of law, there is no doubt that they were describing an aspect of social reality which could be said to fall within the legal 'field' or 'domain'. They saw barristers as 'fully social individual(s) who must satisfy all sorts of competing demands, while at the same time carving out a living from a not particularly welcoming environment'.[12] In advisory work, they wrote, the barrister knows that a client wants a solution to his or her problem, and this means appreciating a large number of factors, including, crucially, costs.[13] They described how barristers assess the likely success of a case by obtaining a 'feel' for its merits (that is, how strong it is on the facts and how far it is consistent with moral feeling) and making a judgment of the law. If the two point in the same direction, the chances are good. If the merits are poor, there is always the risk of losing, even if the law looks favourable. If both law and merits point against the client, it is a 'no hoper'. In engaging with opposing counsel, barristers try to do the best for their client. This might mean 'buying off' a case with poor chance of success (that is, accepting a low offer, which saves everyone the costs of further conflict). Barristers try to discover as much as they can of the character of opposing counsel, since this is helpful in negotiation strategy. They have an interest in being 'fair' and 'straightforward', because someone with a reputation for playing 'dirty' will find negotiation much harder. Good knowledge of procedure is very helpful in negotiation, since much of it is conducted under constraints of time, which is an inherent inhibition against perfect justice.[14] There are seldom conflicts over points of law, requiring legal research. Rather, opposing counsel tend to operate within an agreed legal framework and according to broadly understood principles.[15] In this way, Morison and Leith's work gave a fascinating insight into an important aspect of the experience many people have of the legal system, and therefore, of the law.

II. The Importance of Research

The role of the law in settling family disputes has been a matter of particular debate over the past 25 years. In 1982 the 32nd Report of the

---

[12] Morison and Leith, above n 7, at 19.
[13] *Ibid*, at 106.
[14] *Ibid*, at 123–31.
[15] *Ibid*, at 89–99.

Legal Aid Advisory Committee[16] expressed alarm over the increase in 'ancillary' proceedings (that is, applications and orders for financial and property matters in divorce cases). The Committee did not directly ascribe this development to the role of lawyers, but its suggestion that a remedy might be found through 'conciliation' (the term then used for what is now more usually called 'mediation') implied it. In 1989 the Committee expressly advocated that parties should be encouraged to 'settle their differences without recourse to formal court proceedings' with 'adversarial argument concluded by judgment'.[17] This analysis failed to appreciate that the fact that a court order had been made did not *necessarily* mean that there had been any adversarial argument or court proceedings at all. Most orders were reached by consent after a process of *negotiation* between the parties' lawyers.[18] The reasons why the numbers had increased probably lay in increased property values, wider property ownership, and the greater complexity of arrangements, making their incorporation into a court order desirable.

In 1990, the Law Commission re-examined the law and procedures relating to divorce, and concluded that it would be desirable to replace the 'fault-based' criteria for determining irretrievable breakdown of a marriage with a single condition: effluxion of a specified period of time.[19] The government took this up in the Family Law Act 1996, but injected into the discussion of the proposals its conviction that lawyers aggravated conflict and increased costs. The Act put the new system on the statute book, but the government held back from implementing it until evidence of how it might operate became available. While this evidence was awaited the then Lord Chancellor, Lord Irvine of Lairg, said in a widely reported speech in 1999[20]:

> The Government is determined that as many people as possible know what mediation offers and are given the opportunity to benefit. The agreements reached in mediation have a rational basis. They are the result of constructive negotiations between those concerned. People are able to see that scoring points and settling wrongs, real or imagined, will not be helpful for the future.

Here mediation is contrasted with 'scoring points and settling wrongs, real or imagined', an implicit, but clear, reference to the legal process.

---

[16] HC 189, paras 95–104.
[17] Legal Aid Advisory Committee, 38th Report (1989), HC 134, para 100.
[18] See J Eekelaar, *Regulating Divorce* (Oxford, Clarendon Press, 1991) 27–39.
[19] Law Commission, *The Ground of Divorce*, Law Com No 192 (1990).
[20] Speech at UK Family Law Conference, Cardiff, June 1999.

The government therefore made the promotion of mediation in preference to negotiation through lawyers the key element of its strategy, although the Law Commission had been much more guarded about mediation.[21] This policy was built into the statutory structure of the proposed new divorce system. The process was to be initiated by attendance by one or both parties at an Information Meeting, where, the government said, the 'helpfulness' of mediation would be explained. Apart from certain exempt categories, financial help with public money for legal advice would only be granted if the client first attended a meeting with a mediator to determine whether mediation would be suitable.[22] In January 2001, however, the government abandoned the proposed divorce scheme.[23] It noted that, in its view, the pilot Information Meetings had failed sufficiently to redirect people away from lawyers and toward mediation. In fact, these meetings seemed to have the opposite effect. 39 per cent of those who went to them without contemplating the use of a solicitor had left them convinced that they should see a solicitor, and only six per cent thought they should go to a mediator. Despite this clear evidence of demand for legal assistance, it remains necessary (except in cases where violence is suspected) for a person wanting state funding to assist with legal advice on family law to visit a mediator first, but this is not insisted on unless each party is willing to go.

This was the context in which the research into solicitors' practices in divorce work reported in *Family Lawyers: The Divorce Work of Solicitors* in 2000 was undertaken. That research did not confirm the perception that solicitors 'scored points', obstructed the process of reaching agreement or adopted practices which delayed cases and increased costs. Rather the contrary; it showed that solicitors went to a good deal of trouble 'negotiating a position' with the client which was most likely to achieve a negotiated settlement, within the constraints imposed by the client's interests. They did not always succeed in persuading the client to abandon an unrealistic position, but these tended to be clients with strong grievances who were paying the fee from their own pockets (we referred to these as 'private' clients, to distinguish them from 'publicly-funded' clients). Delays were usually inherent (obtaining the valuation

---

[21] *Looking to the Future: Mediation and the Ground for Divorce, A Consultation Paper* (Cm 2424, 1993) and *Looking to the Future: Mediation and the Ground for Divorce* (Cm 2799, 1995). See the discussion in *Family Lawyers*, above n 1, at 1–9.
[22] Family Law Act 1996 s 29.
[23] Lord Chancellor's Department, Press release, 16 January 2001.

of a property or pension), or a result of intractability of the client, and sometimes constructive. Delay did not always lead to higher costs. If nothing was being done by the lawyers no legal charges would accrue, but other constructive steps might be being taken. The success in eventually achieving orders by consent even in cases of high client hostility was high. Apart from these findings, the research revealed the extremely significant role solicitors played for many clients in helping them manage their finances through an often traumatic period. Far from encouraging parties to divorce, solicitors seemed to advise clients not to proceed unless they were very sure that was their wish.

Despite these findings, the media remained largely critical about the role of lawyers in family law matters, in keeping with the general public lack of confidence in the legal profession.[24] High-profile divorce cases, like that of the McCartneys, sustained perceptions that lawyers aggravate conflict. While the Children and Adoption Bill 2006 was being debated, some of the more extreme fathers' groups, who were not satisfied with the amount of contact fathers were being awarded with their children, claimed that the family justice system is a female conspiracy.[25] In public law, where there had been disquiet arising from the quality and reliability of expert evidence,[26] the restrictions on access by the press and public to courts in children cases led to the expression of concerns from a wide range of individuals and organisations, including senior members of the judiciary, about the lack of transparency in the justice system.[27] The Department for Constitutional Affairs (now the Ministry of Justice) published a Consultation Paper on the matter,[28] which refers to recent developments in other jurisdictions. In New Zealand, for example, the family courts have recently been opened to the accredited press, hoping for a reduction in public criticism about secrecy, but media interest has been slight, mainly because reporting restrictions are stringent.[29] In February 2008, Bridget Prentice, the Parliamentary Under-Secretary of State in the Ministry of Justice,

---

[24] See for example the *New Statesman* special feature 'Are they off their trolley?' (16 February 2004, which began 'How many lawyers does it take to change a light bulb?' to which the answer was 'How many can you afford?'

[25] See Constitutional Affairs Sub Committee, Evidence (March 2006).

[26] The *R v Clark* case and Dr Southall.

[27] See for example, James Munby in evidence on 26 March 2007 to the Constitutional Affairs Select Committee.

[28] *Confidence and Confidentiality; Improving transparency and privacy in the family courts* (London, The Stationery Office, 2006).

[29] J Brophy and C Roberts, *Transparency in the Family Courts, Lessons from other jurisdictions*, Oxford Briefing Paper in press.

announced that the protocol for procedures in public law care cases was to be revised to process cases more quickly. At the same time court fees were increased to over £4,000, which might be construed as a disincentive for a local authority to begin care proceedings.[30]

The climate in which family lawyers practise in England and Wales is therefore a harsh one. There is a firm policy commitment in government to reduce court activity to the bare minimum. The Ministry of Justice, the department with responsibility for the Courts Service, constantly reiterates the belief that courts should be the service of last resort, and that family matters are best dealt with privately, or with the help of advice, mediation or counselling.[31] Cynics may attribute this view to the need to limit, control or at the least account for the rising expenditure on legal aid in family disputes. Following the Carter Report,[32] the government seems determined to pursue a market-based system in which firms compete against each other when tendering for publicly-funded contracts, and the contracts are awarded on the basis of an assessment of the quality, quantity and efficiency of the services to be provided to the client. Small firms are likely to find it difficult to have sufficient throughput of cases to compete against larger firms. The result will probably be a further reduction in the number of solicitors willing to do publicly-funded work, and that provision will become concentrated in the hands of large firms.

Of course any department making requests to the Treasury for resources must show good stewardship of the public purse. But resource constraints are not the whole story. There is a firmly held belief in government and among service providers that private agreements 'empower' the individual, and lead to more lasting arrangements and greater satisfaction than any decision imposed by a court. Whether this is true or not, the conclusion that is drawn, namely, that the legal process is antagonistic to agreement and rests primarily on imposed outcomes, and that access to it should therefore be inhibited, is based on scant evidence. Existing research, such as that reported in *Family Lawyers: The Divorce Work of Solicitors*, suggests that there is very little top-down adjudication in family courts. It seems to indicate that the

---

[30] The number of care applications reported by Wells Street Family Proceedings Court in London fell by over one-third between September 2007 and September 2008.

[31] See *Parental Separation: Children's Needs and Parents' Responsibilities—Next Steps* (Department for Constitutional Affairs, 2005).

[32] Lord Carter of Coles, *Legal Aid: a Market-based approach to reform* (Department for Constitutional Affairs, 2006).

main role of the court is in fact to provide a context which *enables* parties to reach agreement by providing a space where facts must be disclosed, issues identified and evidence tested, with or without expert help from non-legal professionals.[33] It is true that the cases are difficult and many going through it might feel frustrated, but it must be remembered that the disputes which come into the forensic process are usually those where passions run the highest, or communication between the disputants has most seriously broken down. It should not be surprising that those who go to court are more angry and upset even after a resolution of their problem has been achieved than those who have not needed to go to court.

These considerations, therefore, provided an important motivation to re-visit and complete the work we had begun in *Family Lawyers: The Divorce Work of Solicitors*. There we had distinguished between solicitors who dealt with private clients, and solicitors whose cases were funded under the legal aid provisions. There seemed to be concern that the number of the latter was falling sharply. If that is true, people who cannot, or cannot easily, find a solicitor willing to take publicly-funded family law work will therefore either have to deal with the solicitor on a private client basis, try their luck with mediation, or deal with the problem without either mediation or professional legal assistance. And if they do not have a solicitor, they are unlikely to have a barrister, because a barrister, with some limited exceptions, will be instructed by a solicitor.[34] Whether we should be concerned about that depends on knowing what contribution the legal profession makes to people experiencing these disturbances in their family lives.[35] *Family Lawyers: The Divorce Work of Solicitors* provided evidence about the contribution of solicitors. We felt it was now necessary to find out more about the contribution of barristers.

---

[33] See J Brophy, J Jhutti-Johal and C Owen *Significant Harm: Child Protection litigation in a multi-cultural setting* (Department for Constitutional Affairs, 2003) and *Minority ethnic parents, their solicitors and child protection litigation* (Department for Constitutional Affairs, 2005).

[34] See also The Lord Chief Justice's review of the Administration of Justice in the Courts, HC 448 (London, The Stationery Office, 2008) para 14.4, referring to the potential reduction of candidates for the judiciary

III. The Project

With support from the Nuffield Foundation, to which we express our gratitude, we began to collect information about the work of the Family Law Bar. We wished to discover (1) the characteristics of that section of the profession, (2) what its members do, and (3) how their activities contribute to the management or resolution of family disputes. To address the first matter we collected together existing material about the structure of the family law bar. This covers the number of barristers who practise family law to some degree, their level of specialisation, the gender balance and their age profile. To answer questions (2) and (3), we undertook an in-depth examination of the day-to-day activity of members of the family law bar through observation of individual barristers as they performed their role in the context of a court hearing, and conducted a telephone survey in which barristers were asked about their role in their most recent case. We have not included the preparation of written opinions, which is entirely separate from court work, though some of the barristers who were observed were working on cases which settled without the need for going to court, or without the need for adjudication.

The details of the methods employed are described at the appropriate points in the text. As we proceeded with the project, it became clear that we could not expect from counsel an account of the entire progress of a case from the client's point of view. The barrister is not called in until the case reaches a particular stage, and may only do a specific 'job' for the client, rather than seeing a case through to the end. If the solicitor is like the architect who sees the building of a house through from design to completion, the barrister might be likened to the plumber, called in to do a specific job. However a leaking tap may develop into a collapse of the entire heating system, while an apparently disastrous flood may turn out to be no more than a faulty stop-cock. But the information does allow us to address a range of questions. Do we have an excessively adversarial family justice system? Are the financial rewards excessive in 'big money' cases and inadequate in child protection cases? Is the family bar a well-rewarded group profiting unduly from ancillary relief divorce work? Is there a problem of recruitment to a poorly-rewarded, beleaguered, but essential workforce protecting children at risk of harm? Is it still possible to talk of the family bar as single profession? What common ground is there between a provider of luxury services for the rich, and jobbing fixers for troubled families which have no resources?

9

These are some of the questions to be addressed in the following chapters. Chapter two considers the nature of the family law bar: its training and qualifications, levels of specialisation, geographical spread, gender and age distributions, and regulation and remuneration. Chapter three examines the framework of the court process within which barristers operate by analysing information about how a sample of barristers described what they did in relation to their most recent 'hearing'. Chapters four to six draw on observational data, and will look at the day-to-day work of the family law bar in three areas of work: financial cases (both 'big money' and 'small money' cases), private law children cases (which mainly consists of contact and residence disputes) and public law children cases (where the barrister may be representing a local authority, the parents or other relatives or potential carers, the children or the guardian *ad litem*).

IV. Acknowledgments

A project like this depends heavily on the goodwill of others. Many people have been generous in giving their time to help us in many different ways. We are most grateful to those members of the bar who cheerfully allowed themselves to be accompanied to courts by a researcher, and at the end of a long day patiently described what they had been doing, explaining both the mundane and the arcane mysteries of their work. We thank Cate Hemingway for helping us develop the project and Katie Rainscourt for assisting with the survey, reading drafts and giving invaluable advice about detailed aspects of professional practice.

2

The Family Law Bar

I. Introduction

THE DEARTH OF clear and accessible information about family law barristers encourages the stereotypes in general circulation mentioned in the last chapter. This chapter therefore sets out to describe their demographic characteristics in terms of age and gender, and also their qualifications, specialist training, and experience. It will consider whether there is a specialist family law bar, and, if so, how specialised the practice of family law barristers is. Do they do all kinds of family law cases or are they divided into those who concentrate on children cases and those who deal with financial matters? Do practitioners in children cases cover both private law (mostly contact and residence cases) and public law (primarily the protection of children from abuse or neglect)? Do family law barristers combine family cases with other civil cases, or with welfare or benefits work? We will also consider the economic incentives and constraints and the regulatory framework. Is the family law bar divided according to whether the source of funding is the private client or the public purse? Are its practitioners sufficiently remunerated to safeguard adequate levels of recruitment? And, following the review by Sir David Clementi of the regulation of legal services,[1] we will consider how the family law bar is organised and regulated.

II. The Demographic Characteristics of the Family Law Bar

In the absence of a single authoritative source of information, we have drawn on the statistics provided by the Bar Council, the General

---

[1] *Review of the Regulatory Framework for Legal Services in England and Wales*, Report by Sir David Clementi to the Lord Chancellor, December 2004.

Council of the Bar Directory,[2] the websites of individuals and chambers, the extremely informative Survey of the Family Law Bar carried out in 2002 by the Family Law Bar Association (FLBA), and Elizabeth Walsh's *Working in the Family Justice System*, published by *Family Law* in 2006 as the Official Handbook of the Family Justice Council.[3] We have also been helped by the overview of Family Legal Service prepared by the Legal Services Commission in Volume 2 of their strategy paper, *Making Legal Rights a Reality for Children and Families*, published in March 2007, though this focuses mainly on the work of solicitors.[4] Though it is sometimes difficult to piece together information collected for different purposes and at different times, we have found no conflict in the information from these various sources, so we are confident that we have a reasonably accurate picture of the profession.

A. Family Law Chambers

It appears that there are just over 200 sets of chambers where family law business is carried out. The Bar Council Directory, which relies on self reporting, lists 219, and the FLBA Survey, which includes all sets of chambers containing at least one barrister who is a member of the FLBA, gives 215. Family law business is defined as including court work (final hearings, directions or interim hearings, injunctive relief hearings concerned with either domestic violence or financial relief, and on rare occasions a committal hearing or hearing for the enforcement of a financial order), as well as preparatory work (conferences with a client before or after the issue of proceedings, advice in writing or by telephone before or after the issue of proceedings, and paperwork, such as written advice after issue, practice direction documents, and drafting statements or affidavits). The kinds of case include ancillary relief or other financial matters between married or formerly married parties, private law issues concerning children, public law matters involving children, adoption (which contains both private and public law elements), domestic violence, child abduction, divorce, property or other financial matters between cohabitants or former cohabitants, and inheritance. Funding may be on a private client basis, or public (funded

---

[2] *General Council of the Bar Directory*, 2005 edn (London, Thomson, Sweet and Maxwell, 2004).

[3] E Walsh, *Working in the Family Justice System*, 2nd edn (Bristol, Family Law, 2006).

[4] *Making Legal Rights a Reality for Children and Families* (London, Legal Services Commission, 2007).

through the Legal Services Commission (LSC)), or the work may be carried out *pro bono* (without charge). The courts include the Family Proceedings or Magistrates' Courts, the County Court, the High Court, the Divisional Court, the Court of Appeal and the House of Lords.

According to the General Council of the Bar Directory,[5] the chambers where family law is practised are located unevenly across the six court circuits. There are 19 sets of chambers in the Midlands, 38 on the Northern circuit and nine in the North East. The vast majority, 126 sets of chambers, are to be found on the South-Eastern Circuit. There are 12 sets in Wales and Chester and 15 on the Western Circuit. Within the South East, chambers which include family law barristers are concentrated in central London. Table 1 sets out the numbers of chambers which include barristers practising in family law by London postcode.

Table 1

London Postcode	Number of Chambers
EC4	47
WC2	22
WC1	16
W1	2
HA4	1
NW10	1
N22	1
EC1	1
Total	91

Chambers which deal in family law vary in size, from sole practitioners to the largest chambers housing over 150 barristers, where, instead of renting a room, the tenants 'hot desk', using a joint library and clerking system, and plugging their laptops into the common system, thus maintaining their efficiency while considerably reducing their expenses. Table 2 sets out the numbers of chambers of various sizes as described in the Directory. The majority fall into the group comprising more than 20 but less than 50 counsel.

---

5   Above, n 2.

Table 2

Size of Chambers	Number in Directory
1	8
2–10	16
11–19	39
21–50	107
51–80	39
81–100	6
Over 100	6

B. Family Law Barristers

The information which follows on individual barristers is taken from the 2002 FLBA survey which sampled all those barristers practising any family law in all sets of chambers containing at least one barrister who was a member of the FLBA. 155 sets of chambers participated in the survey, including 1,986 individuals who did any family law business, even if very little, as part of their day-to-day practice. Sixty-three barristers were not working at the time of the survey. Of the remaining 1,923, 1,672 responded to the survey, a response rate of 87 per cent for these chambers. Within the 60 sets of chambers that did not participate in the survey, there were only 68 FLBA members, so it is reasonable to suppose that these sets contained only few members who did a substantial amount of family law work

(i) The Gender Balance

The proportion of women barristers practising family law is higher than the proportion of women as a whole at the bar. But it is representative of the proportion of women in the population as a whole. 51 per cent of the 1,672 respondents to the FLBA survey were women. In the bar as a whole, which comprised 14,362 practising barristers, 32 per cent were women. According to the General Council of the Bar's Annual Reports, the gender balance of those called to the bar does reflect that of the general population. In 2004, 49 per cent of those called to the bar were women. But the distribution changes when we look at those who become self-employed. Only 29 per cent of those were women.

(ii) The Age Distribution

It is important to see whether there may be a recruitment problem to the family law bar. If there is, it could become an ageing group, though this could also be seen as a group which has achieved seniority in the profession. Tables 3 and 4 show both the number of years of practice of family law barristers and their status. Examination of other data sources does not reveal any significant difference between family law barristers and the bar as a whole.

Table 3 Family law barristers: by years of practice

Years of practice	Number of barristers	%
1–2	187	11.2
3–5	216	12.9
6–10	294	17.8
11–15	298	17.8
16–20	212	12.7
Over 20	393	23.5
No data	72	4.3
Total	1672	100.2

Table 4 Family law barristers: by seniority of status

Barrister seniority	Number of barristers	%
Pupil or squatter	74	4.4
Less than 4 years since call	259	15.5
4–12 years since call	577	34.5
Over 12 years since call	671	40.0
Queen's Counsel	78	4.7
No data	13	0.8
Total	1672	

C. Recruitment and Training

Those who read for the bar either have a law degree or have passed the Common Professional Examination or obtained the Graduate Diploma in Law, which are intensive one-year courses for graduates in other subjects which prepare the candidate for the professional training. The professional training is through the Bar Vocational Course (BVC). This is provided by a number of establishments, one of the most important being the Inns of Court School of Law, situated within City University, London, which takes on 500 students between May and September each year. There seems to be no reluctance at the training stage to consider working in family law. For example, in 2006 more than half of the students at the Inns of Court School of Law chose family law as one of their two optional subjects for the final examination. Most of the students who chose the family law option combined this with the criminal law paper, rather than with commercial law. Apparently they preferred 'people-based' rather than 'paper-based' subjects. They begin by learning rules and procedures applicable in civil and criminal law. They are then taught the technical skills of conferencing and advocacy. This includes training in how to communicate with the client with clarity and how to establish a rapport and trust, remain flexible, and think laterally. The student needs to understand how a conference with a barrister, who is there to do a specific task, differs from a conference between a client and the solicitor, who is there to see a case through from beginning to end. The students are taught about evidence and styles of questioning. They learn about various ways of listening to the client. These include the passive mode, where the client retains control and is not interrupted, the responsive mode, where the advocate supports the flow of narrative, the receptive mode, where the barrister offers some emotional response and support, and active listening, where the listener offers a summary which will include an element of value judgment about what has been said. There are exercises in 'fact management', drafting, note-taking and giving advice orally and as a written opinion. This is followed by advocacy training, which deals with styles of questioning, setting of the 'advocacy trap' to secure the most useful answer, and training in negotiation. Having acquired the necessary professional skills and techniques, the students choose two options. As we have noted, it seems that more than half of the students usually choose family law, often taken with criminal law. Both of these require face-to-face interaction with clients rather than the mainly paper-based work of commercial practice. Problem-based seminars are held for small groups. But because family law cases need to be considered on their facts rather than on legal rules alone, this is the only option examined both on paper, and through practical tests.

What are these students' career expectations and opportunities? A few have places in chambers at the established family law sets before coming on the course. But anecdotal evidence suggests that it is hard for those who want to practise family law in a less specialised set of chambers to find a place, although it may not be any harder in family law than in other specialised areas.

III. Specialisation

We now examine the extent to which family law barristers specialise. Specialisation can take two forms. One reflects the time spent on family law matters as distinct from other branches of legal practice. The other concerns specialisation within family law itself. As regards the first ('external specialisation'), the FLBA Survey showed that seven out of ten barristers in chambers where there was a FLBA member spent more than half their time on family law business (Table 5).

Table 5 Time spent on family law business

More than 50 %	1165	69.7 %
Less than 50 %	491	29.4 %
No data	13	0.8 %

Where the barrister described himself or herself as spending over half their time on family law matters, the distribution between ancillary relief, public law children cases and other family law work was as follows (Table 6).

Table 6 Specialisation within family law

Ancillary relief (financial)	164	14 %
Children (public law)	282	24 %
Family general	707	60.7 %
No information	13	1.1 %

So we can see a well-defined specialist group of barristers who specialise in family law. Almost 70 per cent of those in chambers with an FLBA member spent over half their time on family law. Most of these (61 per cent) will do a general range of family law work, but some concentrate on particular fields within family law: 24 per cent on child protection and 14 per cent on ancillary relief (financial matters). The Bar Directory also indicates the presence of a small group who combine family law practice with practice in welfare, housing and immigration law; an interesting reflection of the need of many people for help with a number of problems which may well be interrelated. A health problem may lead to unemployment, debt, housing issues and relationship breakdown. In its work on paths to justice, the LSC Research Centre describes this as 'problem clustering'.[6] It is particularly difficult for the legal system to respond to these needs in a holistic way, because the nature of the legal process tends to break issues down into discrete segments. Family law, however, inclines to emphasise the future needs of those concerned rather than past behaviour and is better placed to try to develop a more inclusive approach.

When the family law bar is compared with solicitors who practise family law, we find that their profile is remarkably similar. Women are well represented in both branches of the profession, though the view that family law is a female preserve may arise from public contact with family lawyers practising as solicitors rather than as barristers, as women are over-represented in that group.[7] Both branches of the profession include substantial numbers of members in the older age range. The solicitors included many with income levels below those of their peers working in other areas of law. We are not able to make such a statement with confidence about the bar, but anecdotally it seems likely to be the case, with the possible exception of barristers specialising in 'big money' cases. The degree of specialisation is similar across the two branches of the profession. The Law Society reported that although 75 per cent of solicitors' firms with less than 80 partners offered family law services, in practice the bulk of the work is carried out by specialists, defined as those who spend at least 50 per cent of their time on it. For these 2,600 female and 1,300 male family law solicitors, this is the least profitable area of activity, and gender reduces earnings by an average of £6,000 a year for women.[8] In addition, the specialists are on the whole

---

[6] P Pleasence, *Civil Law and Social Justice* (London, The Stationery Office, 2006); see also R Moorhead and M Robinson, *A trouble shared: legal problem clustering in Solicitors and Advice Agencies* (Department for Constitutional Affairs, 2006).

[7] Drawing on the Law Society Panel Study of 500 firms and on the Omnibus survey of 700 individual practitioners, John Eekelaar, Mavis Maclean and Sarah Beinart found that two out of three family specialist solicitors were women. *Family Lawyers: The Divorce Work of Solicitors* (Oxford, Hart Publishing, 2000) ch 3.

[8] B Cole and J Siddaway, *A study of Private Practice Solicitors* (RPPU Paper no 24, 1997) and B Cole, *Solicitors in Private Practice: their work and expectations, Research Study no 26* (Law Society, 1997).

older than those who do not specialise. So, across both branches of the profession, there is cause for concern about levels of recruitment to a specialist branch of legal service, for which demand shows no sign of diminishing.

Even if the need for support in divorce may fall as the marriage and divorce rates decline,[9] the need for help in cases of separation between unmarried cohabitants is likely to increase. The Law Commission has recommended legislation to provide a basis for dealing with property and financial issues that may arise when unmarried partners separate.[10] The government, however, has decided to await evidence from similar Scottish legislation[11] before taking a position on this.[12] But whether legislative action is taken or not, legal problems will continue to arise in those circumstances. And in public law the need for specialist legal help with care proceedings shows no signs of diminishing. The government has accepted that parents should receive additional financial assistance when a local authority decides to bring proceedings.[13]

IV. Remuneration and Regulation of the Family Law Bar

A. The Changing Face of Legal Aid in Family Law Cases

In the most recent Strategy Plan for 2004–09 *Delivering Justice, Rights and Democracy*[14] the Ministry of Justice (then the Department for Constitutional Affairs) referred to concerns about the coverage of legal need in some parts of the country. To understand the current situation it is helpful to recall the recent history of the development of public funding for legal services. The origins of the legal aid scheme lie in the need to help ex service men and women to divorce in the period

---

[9] In 2006 the number of divorces fell by 7% from the number in 2005 (Office of National Statistics, online).

[10] Law Commission, *Cohabitation: the financial consequences of relationship breakdown* (Cm 7182, 2007).

[11] Family Law (Scotland) Act 2006.

[12] Statement by Bridget Prentice, Under-Secretary of State in the Ministry of Justice, 6 March 2008.

[13] See *The Review of the Child Care Proceedings System in England and Wales* (Department for Constitutional Affairs and Department for Children, Schools and Families, 2006)

[14] *Delivering Rights, Justice and Democracy* (London, Department for Constitutional Affairs, 2004) 26.

immediately after the Second World War, when a large number of marriages contracted in haste or struggling with the impact of separation and harsh conditions failed, and it was felt that the government had a responsibility to support the men and women involved.[15] In the foreword to their reader on *Resourcing Civil Justice*[16] Tamara Goriely and Alan Paterson refer to the famous essay on Citizenship and Social Class given as a lecture in Cambridge by Professor TH Marshall, where he cited the Legal Advice and Assistance Bill 1949 as completing the project started in the eighteenth century to provide the full and equal exercise of civil rights. The legal profession did not instigate the scheme. The Law Society came to support it only reluctantly.[17] But the breakdown of the charitable pro bono system created a political impetus evidenced by letters to MPs, concerns expressed by social welfare groups, and articles by academics. The Law Society originally rejected plans for a paid legal aid system, only accepting the proposal when the lack of help for divorcing parties could no longer be ignored. The profession does not seem to have been aiming to create a new area of business.[18] Similarly, the calls for improved access to legal services which developed in the 1960s and 1970s came from a wide spectrum of groups with different motivations, not only the legal profession. The argument that demand for legal services has been supplier-led is less convincing than the alternative: that demand for legal help in family matters has grown with increasingly complex legislation, and the growth in capital assets held by those seeking to end a marriage and unpick their joint finances.

By the time of retrenchment in public expenditure in the late 1980s and early 1990s, the rise in legal aid expenditure gave the government serious cause for concern. Legal aid expenditure had doubled between 1990 and 1995, reaching a total of £1.4 billion in 1995–96. Demand seemed infinite and resources finite. The government took ad hoc defensive measures. It raised eligibility levels and staging payments,[19] and then introduced a franchising system for services. The review of

---

[15] See S Cretney, *Family Law in the Twentieth Century: A History* (Oxford, Oxford University Press, 2003) 309–18.

[16] T Goriely and A Paterson, *Resourcing Civil Justice* (Oxford, Oxford University Press, 1996)

[17] See M Maclean in S Katz, J Eekelaar and M Maclean (eds), *Cross Currents: Family Law and Policy in the US and England* (Oxford, Oxford University Press, 2001) ch 18.

[18] See Goriely and Paterson, above n 16, at 3–4.

[19] See the *Scrutiny Review* (Lord Chancellor's Department, 1988) and the *Staged Payments Review* (Lord Chancellor's Department, 1991).

expenditure on legal services in 1993–94 culminated in the Green Paper *Legal Aid: Targeting Need*[20] and the White Paper, *Striking the Balance: the future of legal aid in England and Wales.*[21] These led to the Access to Justice Act 1999. The policy was to cap the legal aid fund, look to non-lawyers for certain services, reduce eligibility for some parts of civil work and increase contributions of recipients of legal aid to their legal costs. An important mechanism for restraining expenditure was the introduction of the Family Graduated Fees Scheme (FGFS), whereby payment, which had previously been made according to time spent, was replaced by fees graduated according to the complexity of the specific tasks done.

As explained in the previous chapter, in family law the policy of trying to divert people away from courts and lawyers had already emerged in the Family Law Act 1996. This sought to direct divorcing parties away from lawyers and courts towards alternative dispute resolution in the form of mediation and to encourage consensual clean-break settlements.[22] It was thought that this would offer the double advantage of saving money (as it was widely assumed that mediation would be far cheaper than courts and lawyers), and of doing the parties good by empowering them to take charge of their lives and reach their own agreements. But these hopes were not fulfilled. The cost of mediation on a national scale was hard to quantify, as mediation services had largely developed as not-for-profit agencies. The start-up costs for the newly expanding pilot services were higher than expected,[23] while demand remained low. It is difficult to obtain figures for the private sector, but for publicly-funded mediation, even 10 years later (2006), the Legal Services Commission reported support to only 14,000 mediations.[24] The Office of National Statistics' Online Divorce Statistics 2007 report 141,750 divorces for 2005, and the figure for couples experiencing relationship breakdown would be far higher if it included those separating after cohabitation. On the other hand, greater public responsibility was assumed for child support. The Child Support Act 1991 largely transferred the assessment and implementation of child maintenance to an administrative agency, partly to allay calls on the benefits

---

[20] *Legal Aid: Targeting Need* (Cm 2854, 1995).

[21] *Striking the Balance: the future of legal aid in England and Wales* (Cm 3305, 1996).

[22] J Eekelaar in S Katz, J Eekelaar and M Maclean (eds), *Cross Currents*, above n 17, ch 18.

[23] See G Davis, G Bevan and LSC Staff, *Monitoring Publicly Funded Mediation*, Report to the Legal Services Commission (2000).

[24] *Making Legal Rights a Reality for Children and Families*, above n 4, at para 2.47.

system from the increasing number of lone parents, but also to impose this financial responsibility on non-resident parents and to take the issue of setting child maintenance out of the hands of lawyers and courts.[25]

Despite these changes, substantial public funding for family law work has remained, particularly in public law children cases. The total spend rose from £405,649,684 in 2002–03 to £511,120,137 in 2005–06.[26] But government concerns about the level of spending were exacerbated by the way spending was increasing at a faster rate than the volume of cases. Spending increased by 12 per cent between 2004–05 and 2005–06, compared to a 2.6 per cent rise in case volume. In July 2006 further reforms to the legal aid system were proposed by Lord Carter of Coles.[27] The ultimate goal seems to be a 'market-based' system in which firms of solicitors are to compete against each other when tendering for public funding, the funding is granted on the basis of an assessment of the quality, quantity and efficiency of the services to be provided to the client, and fixed fees will be eventually determined by the service provided.[28] Until then, as a transitional stage, funding will be based on standardised fees for certain types of advice, and graduated fees, as amended in 2007, will remain for the various stages of legal process. The most probable outcome of the new approach, though, is that publicly-funded work will only be sustainable by firms which can turn over a large number of cases. The firms providing it will become larger and fewer, and therefore less accessible. Lord Carter made no specific recommendations for change in the way the family bar was remunerated. But the government has revisited the matter, and in a letter to *The Times* on 21 May 2008 the Minister with responsibility for legal aid, Lord Hunt stated that 'currently barrister family advocates are paid much more than solicitor family advocates for the same work … we want a fairer system where they are paid the same'. He then confirmed plans to consult on proposals to reduce payments to family barristers either directly or by removing some of the more complex elements of the payments scheme. The most recent figures for the proportion of publicly-funded cases in which solicitors instruct counsel are 38 per

---

[25] For a full account, see N Wikeley, *Child Support: Law and Policy* (Oxford, Hart Publishing, 2006).

[26] *Making Legal Rights a Reality for Children and Families*, above n 4, at 20.

[27] Lord Carter of Coles, *Legal Aid: a market based approach to reform* (Department of Constitutional Affairs, July 2006)

[28] *Ibid*, at ch 2.

cent for Special Children Act cases,[29] at an average cost of £4,880, and 40 per cent for private law children cases at an average cost of £1,380.[30]

The respondents to the FLBA survey have clearly been concerned about the climate of policy towards family law practice for some time. In 2002, 75 per cent of the specialists at the family law bar reported low morale, and 20 per cent were thinking of giving up family work altogether, especially the older practitioners. Furthermore, 10 per cent (105 out of the 1,513) of those doing legal aid work had stopped and attributed this to the graduated fee scheme. The rate of withdrawal varied according to specialism within the family law community. 42 per cent of the 155 ancillary relief specialists stopped taking on legally aided work, compared to three per cent of the 270 doing children public law cases. Four per cent of the remaining 681 specialist family law bar respondents had stopped taking on legal aid cases. The FLBA remains concerned that, without additional funding and substantial restructuring, the family law bar will be depleted and the publicly-funded client will find him or herself without the level of representation needed particularly in the complex cases. The family law bar believe that their publicly-funded activities concern the most disadvantaged members of society at a stage where crucial decisions are made affecting their rights to family life, and that it is important that this is done by specialist and experienced practitioners. They argue that there can be serious consequences if the work is done by those who do not have the necessary skill and experience. For example, delay in reaching a decision about the future of a child involved in care proceedings is widely held to be a matter of concern. It is the expert advice and assistance of the family law bar which enables the key issues to be identified early on (these may not be the issues identified by the parties involved) so that courts can avoid spending time on matters which are not relevant, and cases can be resolved before a final hearing.

In his evidence to the Constitutional Affairs Select Committee in May 2006, the President of the Family Division, Sir Mark Potter, argued that he hoped to see more family law business going to the Family Proceedings Courts, which are currently under-used, in order to relieve the pressure on the County Courts.[31] If this happens, the contribution of experienced specialist members of the bar in assisting the lay magistracy—who have had some training in family matters but lack the

---

[29] Special Children Act cases are those which are non-means-tested and largely non-merits-tested for the key parties in the most significant childcare proceedings
[30] *Making Legal Rights a Reality for Children and Families*, above n 4, at para 2.17.
[31] Evidence to the Constitutional Affairs Select Committee, 2 May 2006.

specialist knowledge and experience of the judges in the County Courts—will become even more important. Similarly, although it is hoped that fewer financial matters will come to court as alternative methods of dispute management become more popular, it is still only the court which has the power to compel disclosure of assets, often the key obstacle to reaching an appropriate settlement. Concerns have been raised with the Legal Services Commission about the practice whereby publicly-funded work is not carried out by senior members of a firm because of the relatively low rate of remuneration but is handed to the most junior (so-called 'juniorisation'). The LSC quite properly wants to avoid paying the most expensive members of the profession to carry out relatively simple tasks. But if 'juniorisation' is taken too far it may reduce efficiency and set up a vicious circle in which the LSC is disappointed in the time taken to complete a task, and the lawyers' arguments for any increase in rates of pay become hard to make.

B. Remuneration levels

In our survey reported in the next chapter, we observed that fees for private clients in family law work are arrived at in a number of ways. In some cases they are described as being negotiated with regard to the means of the client. Methods seem to vary. Sometimes travel costs are not charged, at least for short journeys. In one instance, half the hourly rate was charged for a long journey while a full charge was made for work done for a different client during the journey. Some barristers did their own clerking, some left negotiations to the clerk on a unit basis or an hourly rate. Another factor might be whether the barrister wished to work again for the instructing solicitor. Payment was not always prompt.

As regards publicly-funded fees, the 2002 FLBA survey provides detailed information on the hourly rates of remuneration for different kinds of work and also by level of court. The data were prepared by considering each chargeable unit of work and adding up the total amount of time the survey respondent actually took to complete it. The amount paid for the unit was then converted into an hourly rate in order to allow comparisons to be made between the different remuneration arrangements. The analysis in the survey compares the levels of private fees, legal aid fees under the previous system and the newly introduced graduated fees paid for ancillary relief and other financial matters, private law children work, public law children work, and domestic violence cases. The report also compares the brief fee for the first day of trial, refreshers for second or subsequent days, those for directions or interim hearings other than injunctions, committals, and conferences or written advice after issue. These categories cover eight out of ten cases. The findings show that in all categories the new graduated fee scheme is markedly less generous than the earlier legal aid rates for any second or subsequent day of a trial, any interim or directions hearings, conference after issue and written advice after issue. Priority is given to frontloading to move the case out of court as quickly as possible.

The FLBA survey gives information about differences in rates of public funding for barristers at different stages in their career and in the different parts of the courts service. It was surprising to see that 20 per cent of barristers who conducted cases under the new graduated fee scheme in 2002 were paid at less than £26 an hour, 30 per cent, less than £33 and 40 per cent, less than £40 per hour. Given the tax burden and the costs of membership of chambers, travel expenses and so on, it is hardly surprising that there are concerns about the willingness of barristers to continue to undertake this kind of work. However, the graduated fee scheme has reduced the variations in rates of pay at different levels of court. For example, the median hourly rate for a barrister under the scheme is £45 in the Family Proceedings Court and £46 in the County Court, compared to £68 in the Family Proceedings Court and £77 in the County Court under the previous legal aid scheme. The comparable fees for private clients were £64 and £97. The scheme seems to be prioritising child protection and domestic violence cases, offering incentives to spend the shortest possible time in court, and to reduce the differences between payment in the different courts.

The fact that financial cases are the least well rewarded under the FGFS, and public law cases the best rewarded, could account for the levels of stress and withdrawal from financial work but a far lower rate of withdrawal from public law children work. This is particularly striking because it is commonly thought that involvement in child protection cases is particularly stressful. Yet the anxieties caused by reduction in legal aid for financial cases seem to have driven more barristers from that area of practice. The impact has been more severe on junior members of the profession than on their senior colleagues. For example, the hourly rate for a QC, which had been £192 under the previous legal aid scheme, now became £161 (a 16 per cent reduction), whereas for a junior of more than 12 years call the previous amount of £74 under the old scheme has been reduced to £50 under the new (a 32 per cent reduction).

The data from our survey reported in the next chapter shows that in publicly funded cases, counsel were generally paid under the revised FGFS. The purpose of the scheme is to provide certainty, so the amount is pre-determined. The payments vary according to the nature of the work, which is divided into five functions:

> F1: Pre-litigation, advisory and drafting falling outside other functions.
> F2: Applications for injunctive relief or enforcement procedures.
> F3: Preliminary applications, interim injunctions and review hearings.
> F4: Conferences.
> F5: The main hearing.

The fee may be supplemented according to special issues or court bundles. The prescriptive nature of the scheme is such that counsel may be generously rewarded in some areas and less so in others. They appear to apply best in care cases which are lengthy, organised according to a strict protocol, and involve multiple hearings. A standard financial case will have a maximum of three hearings, the first two of which will be viewed by the LSC as interim hearings, although there is an uplift element for Financial Dispute Resolution (FDR) and settlement. The vast majority of cases settle at FDR, and these require a good deal of expertise to achieve. Under the FGFS, if an FDR takes all day and settlement is reached at 5.15 pm, two and a half hearing units are due under F3, category 4 (£120 x 2.5) plus settlement uplift of 50 per cent of one unit (£60) plus FDR uplift. The total is some £420. This is very different from fees charged to private clients for similar work, which, in our survey, ranged from £800 plus VAT for an FDR to £1,750 plus VAT for a First Appointment/FDR.

Two barristers complained that the LSC had limited the number of conferences to two, leaving counsel in a difficult position if they need to review the case with the client at the end of the day as they will not be paid for this. Barristers doing public work seemed to accept with resignation that they had very little control over when they would be paid. 'Your guess is as good as mine' one answered when asked when he expected payment. Another said: 'I was often taxed down for no reason that is explainable by the LSC. There are some hearings which are delayed in payment when others are more quick ... there seems no rhyme or reason'.

C. Regulation

As well as experiencing increasingly rigorous governmental monitoring of public funding, and the denigration of advocacy as compared to the promotion of alternative methods of dispute resolution,[32] the family law bar, with the bar as a whole, is in the midst of significant changes with respect to professional practice and regulation. Since the government is trying to make professional services more consumer-oriented, it has a strong interest in moving away from practices associated with traditional professional control and exploring new ways in which complaints about the service received from lawyers might be reduced and dealt with, and also how the public might access legal help. In this context it is also addressing concerns that have been expressed about the secrecy of the family justice system.

In 2003 the Department for Constitutional Affairs asked Sir David Clementi to 'consider what regulatory framework would best promote competition, innovation and the public and consumer interest in an efficient, effective and independent legal sector'; and to 'recommend a framework which will be independent in representing the public and consumer interest, comprehensive, accountable, consistent, flexible, transparent and no more restrictive or burdensome than is clearly justified'. Sir David reported in 2004.[33] In his Foreword, Sir David noted that the word 'independent' appeared twice in the terms of reference, and that he regarded this as referring to regulation being independent both of government and of those being regulated. Each of those was important.[34] Self-regulation has traditionally been regarded as essential by the established professions, but it is often brought into question when confidence in the profession is shaken. For example, it has long been as an issue in medicine.[35] But the work of the LSE Centre for the

---

[32] See also R Moorhead, 'Legal Aid and the declines of private practice: blue murder or toxic shock' (2004) 11 *International Journal of the Legal Profession* 159–90.

[33] D Clementi, *Review of the Regulatory Framework for Legal Services in England and Wales: Final Report* (December 2004).

[34] *Ibid*, foreword, para 5.

[35] See The *Report of the Public Inquiry into children's heart surgery at the Bristol Royal Infirmary 1984–1995* (Cm 5207, 2001) 442.

Analysis of Risk and Regulation shows that it may not be helpful to draw a clear distinction between self-regulation and regulation by others, but instead to see the strands as interconnected.[36] While only self-regulation can provide the depth of understanding of the work of the profession, only an injection of independent scrutiny can satisfy external concerns about self interest and closed doors where regulation is seen to be an adjunct of representation of the group's interests.

Traditionally, complaints have been dealt with by the Bar Council under the headings of inadequate professional service, professional misconduct and negligence. In addition complaints may be taken a stage further to the Legal Services Ombudsman, established in 1990, and, since February 2004, to the Legal Services Complaints Commissioner.[37] But the Clementi Report recommended setting up a single system of regulation for both solicitors and barristers operating under an supervisory regulator, the Legal Services Board.[38] There should be a single complaints organisation acting under the supervision of the Board, the Office of Legal Complaints.[39] The cost is estimated at approximately £6 million.[40] The conclusions of the report were largely accepted by the government and incorporated in the Legal Services Act 2007.

In addition, the Act provides for the introduction of Alternative Business Structures, which remove a number of restrictions and enable a variety of legal and non-legal services to be provided in a single setting. The longer-term effects of these changes remain to be experienced. They will, however, add to the stresses of practice at the family law bar, and contribute to the atmosphere of official scepticism about the value of its role.

The final strand of government policy with respect to the legal profession arose from expressions of lack of public confidence in the family justice system and calls to end the culture of secrecy by opening up the family courts to press and or the public. Following cases where the expert evidence of the paediatricians Professor Sir Roy Meadow and

---

[36] R Baldwin, B Hutter and H Rothstein, *Risk Regulation, Management and Compliance* (2000) referred to in Annex B of *Learning from Bristol* (Cm 5071, July 2001) available on the BRI website.

[37] The latter overlaps significantly with the former and appears to have been an interim measure pending the outcome of the Clementi review: *Clementi Report*, above n 33, Chapter C—Complaints and Discipline, para 31

[38] *Clementi Report*, above n 33, Chapter A—Objectives and Principles, paras 70–71.

[39] *Clementi Report*, above n 33, Chapter C—Complaints and Discipline, para 46.

[40] *Clementi Report*, above n 33, Chapter C—Complaints and Discipline, para 85.

Dr David Southall was discredited, and also the expression of anger by some extreme groups, such as Fathers4Justice, representing the interests of fathers who fail to achieve the kind of contact orders which they had sought, the Ministry of Justice published a Consultation Paper, *Confidence and Confidentiality: Improving transparency and privacy in family courts*. This focused on the principle that the best way to achieve openness in the family courts was to allow the media access as of right.

But the response to the Consultation Paper from children and families, as well from the legal and other professionals who support them, was that this would pose a fundamental risk to their privacy and welfare. In the second Consultation Paper, *Openness in the family courts: a new approach*, in June 2007,[41] Lord Falconer, the then Lord Chancellor, announced that he had decided against giving the media access as of right. Instead, the focus would be on the flow of information out of the family courts. A pilot scheme to make anonymised judgments available on a website and directly to parties will begin in three areas in the autumn of 2008, and hopefully public understanding of and confidence in what happens in court, including the contribution made by the family law bar, will improve.

---

[41] *Openness in the family courts: a new approach* (Ministry of Justice, 2007) http://www.dca.gov.uk/consult/courttransparency1106/response-cp.pdf

3

Overview of the Barristers' Role

I. Introduction

WE HAVE LOOKED in detail at the make up of the family law bar, and the regulatory and policy context in which its members operate. We now wish to describe the nature of the work family law barristers do, both the range of cases in which they become involved and the specific tasks and skills they use. We will begin in this chapter by giving a relatively broad overview based on interviews with 36 barristers of the range of cases in which they are instructed, and how their contributions fit in to the handling of the case within the legal system. We include information about their remuneration for the contribution described, wherever possible. The information given related to gross fees, which exclude chambers expenses (usually 20 per cent of the gross fee).[1] It was not the purpose of these interviews to elicit detailed information about the day-to-day activities of the barristers. The information in the present chapter therefore should be seen as setting out the broader framework in which the activities described in detail in the next chapters take place.

As a barrister is not always involved in a case from its beginning to the end, it was not possible to track the histories of specific cases, as we had done in our study of family law solicitors. The barrister is usually called in when the solicitor is unable to get any further, and is obliged to consider going to court, and prefers to use a barrister even though he may himself have rights of audience. Furthermore, a barrister may be asked to work on a case a number of times during its course, or may take over from another barrister half way through, or may deal with only a small part of the whole picture. As we have suggested earlier, he

---

[1] Fee income also has to meet the costs of any 'fringe benefits' such as sick pay, holiday pay and private pension contributions.

31

or she may be seen as rather like a plumber, called in to provide a particular specialist service in a larger overall building project. So, although barristers talk about a 'case', they tend to mean only the specific part of the matter with which they were involved. Of the barristers who were interviewed, a third had not been the first counsel to be briefed on the case.

Since, as we have said, we wished to exclude purely advisory or preparatory work from our survey, we asked our interviewees to describe to us their involvement in the most recent case in which they *attended court*. This does not mean that there was necessarily an adjudication, or even that the matter came before a judge. It might have been postponed or settled without either occurring. Nevertheless, for convenience, we preferred to use the term 'hearing' to describe the matter upon which we gathered our information, even when the matter was dealt with without a presentation to a judge. This is partly because they usually were 'hearings' of some kind, but also because the court attendance required each side to clarify their position and allowed each party, or their lawyer, to hear the other's point of view.

Our data collection instrument was developed through piloting to cover what the barrister had done for his or her last 'hearing' in a form which was suitable to all kinds of work, and designed not to take too much of counsel's time. It was hoped to interview counsel in person, but this proved impractical in view of their unpredictable work assignments, and extensive travelling. But we found a willingness to respond by telephone, supplemented by email. The barristers were requested to cast their minds back to their most recent 'hearing' and were then asked the following questions:

— What kind of case was this?
— Was the case publicly funded?
— Whom did you represent?
— When did the case first come to your attention, and how?
— Were you the first counsel to appear on the case?
— When did the papers reach you? Were they complete? Do you often work for the instructing solicitor?
— How many hours of preparation were required on the papers?
— Did you hold a conference with the solicitor, client, QC or junior? If so, how often, and where did these take place?
— In which court was the hearing listed?
— What kind of hearing was this?
— What was the outcome of the hearing?

— Will you be involved in the case further?

— What was the brief fee and has it been paid? If not paid, when do you expect payment?

We contacted barristers who listed themselves as being in family law practice in the Bar Directory for 2006. We approached 76 barristers listed, but avoided those who helped us with the observational part of the study, reported later, and those who were doing family provision (inheritance) rather than Children Act or ancillary relief work. Only two of the barristers approached expressly refused to help us, but a number of barristers were simply so busy that we never managed to complete the interview despite their willingness to participate. We report data collected in phone and email interviews with 36 barristers. Counsel who choose to be listed in the Directory are self selected, but we were able to test for any distortion in our sample by comparing our achieved sample with the information available from the FLBA survey referred to in chapter two.

Although the numbers are small, the results were encouraging. 17 men and 19 women were interviewed. Of these, three were QCs (two male and one female). 20 (four men and 16 women) had a base outside London, though some of these were members of satellite chambers headed from London. Our gender ratio is close to the national FLBA picture, as is the proportion of those based in London. 41 per cent of the 91 chambers in the FBLA survey were in London, compared to 16 (just under half) of our total of 36 individual respondents who were based in London. But with regard to levels of seniority, the proportion of QCs (nearly eight per cent) is higher than the five per cent in the FLBA survey.

As to the kind of work described to us, in the FLBA sample, 14 per cent of counsel who described themselves as spending more than half their time on family law said they did ancillary relief matters, 24 per cent worked on public law children cases, and 61 per cent on family law in general. We cannot make a direct comparison with our sample as we were asking only about one case, and although some were specialists within family law, those who were generalist family law barristers would have been working on a variety of case types. Of the 36 cases described to us, 14 concerned ancillary relief, 14 were public law children cases (two of which had started as private law actions and there was one committal for breach of an injunction) and eight were private law children cases. All the parties in care cases (excluding the local authorities) were publicly funded, as were five of the private law children cases and three of the ancillary relief cases.

II. Public Law Children Cases (14 Cases, Including A Committal)

Our sample of counsel acting in public law children cases was similar to the larger FLBA survey findings as regards location, gender, and degree of seniority of barristers doing this kind of work. Nine of the barristers were based outside London, including counsel from Oxford, Chester, Cardiff, Leicester, Exeter, Southampton and Manchester. Five were women. Three were QCs (one woman, two men). Two had been called in the 1970s, four in the 1980s, six in the 1990s and two after 2000.

The majority of our sample were representing parents, rather than the local authority or the children. Four were for the mother, four for the father, one for both parents, and one for a maternal grandmother. We have information from only two counsel acting for the local authority and two for the guardian. According to the Legal Services Commission's (LSC) strategy paper,[2] counsel were used in 38 per cent of publicly-funded Special Children Act cases and 35 per cent of other public law children cases, at an average cost of £4,882 in Special Children Act cases and £3,326 in other public law Children Act cases

A. Range of Cases

The 14 barristers who gave us information on care proceedings reported on a wide variety of kinds of case. All were difficult and distressing. We present the information given to us by counsel according to the kind of client represented, beginning with mothers. The variety of work done was striking. Cases included a teenage mother, a bereaved grandmother, allegations of abuse, and an appeal against a care order. There was, however, a consistent message. In these proceedings parents were represented by experienced and committed individuals, who did not appear

---

[2] *Making Legal Rights a Reality for Children and Families* (Legal Services Commission, 2007) 23.

to be dissatisfied with their remuneration, though they were inconvenienced by the time taken for bills to be paid.

(i) Representing Mothers (4 Cases)

In the first case (11), a female barrister of 10 years call, working outside London, described a directions hearing in a case in which she had been acting for a mother with learning difficulties since 2003. The papers were received two weeks ahead of the hearing and in good order from a solicitor with whom she had worked for many years. The fee will be under the Family Graduated Fees Scheme (FGFS), and will be met 'slowly'. There were a number of conferences, but only one will be paid for by LSC. In this case, as in a number of cases, counsel did not know the exact fee for a legally aided case, but received cheques from the LSC periodically which covered more than one case. These fees can now be claimed directly from the LSC by clerks, instead of having to wait to claim via the instructing solicitor. The slow and gradual progress of this case, from private law to care proceedings, reaching a directions hearing after three years, indicates the complexity of the issues which can arise where a parent has learning difficulties and the child protection system has to reconcile the interests of the child with the legal rights of parents.

In the next case (16), a female barrister of 30 years call, working outside London, had been acting for a 16-year-old mother following an application for a placement order for her baby. All parties were publicly funded. The instructing solicitor was not someone she had worked with before, and the papers had not been in good order (for example, the photocopying was deficient). Counsel had held two telephone conferences with the solicitor, and another with the client, on the morning of the hearing and there had been discussion throughout the day. The case was listed to last for three days, and finished in two. Her brief fee was £1,605.

The third case (18) involved a QC, called in 1980, based outside London. He had appeared for the mother in the Court of Appeal, seeking to overturn a care order. He knew the instructing solicitor, from whom the papers had arrived gradually over the preceding month. He had held one conference and prepared a lengthy skeleton argument. The fee was £7,500, which was expected to be paid by the LSC in six months or so.

The fourth case (34) was an eight-day final hearing (which had been listed for seven days), where a residence order was made in favour of the grandmother. The female barrister of 15 years call, based in London, represented the mother. She had worked with the solicitor for many years. The brief fee, calculated in accordance with the FGFS, would be £7,000 which she would expect to receive in about four months time. She commented that

> for hearings such as this the remuneration is very good, but note that hearings such as these almost inevitably involve vulnerable adults who are facing the loss of their children and who are, in my opinion, entitled to representation at an experienced level.

(ii) Representing Fathers (4 Cases)

The cases where our barristers were acting for fathers appear to have involved a more trial-like process than those concerning mothers. Two of these cases involved findings of fact hearings, and one an emergency committal.

In the first finding of fact case (3), a male QC acted for a father in an appeal before a district judge in the Principal Registry to the Family Division against a finding of fact concerning an accusation of sexual abuse. It was listed for three days in court (one for judicial reading, one for oral argument and one for judgment). The appeal was allowed. This client was not legally aided when the case began, but an application had been made to the LSC. The brief fee for the QC was £8,000, but he had not yet been paid pending this application. Although the papers had been in good order, and counsel had been involved in the earlier hearing, the case still required 40 hours of preparation. An hourly rate of £125 has been imputed, in marked contrast to the £55 per hour in case (1), described below, where counsel acting for the guardian was paid by public funds.

The second finding of fact case (19) concerned the threshold criteria[3] in care proceedings. The barrister was from outside London and of less than 10 years call. Agreement was reached, and payment was expected as part of the monthly legal aid cheque, but he could not remember the amount. In the most urgent case (31), a male barrister outside London, called over 25 years ago, acted for the father on public funding for an emergency application to commit for breach of an injunction in a case arising from care proceedings. The papers had arrived at 5.45 pm the previous day. Some documents were missing, but the solicitor had sent a clerk so that the barrister could look at the solicitor's file, and the

---

[3] These are the conditions which must be established if a care, or other intervention order, is to be made: Children Act 1989 s 31.

outcome was a suspended prison sentence. The fee in this case was £310. There may be further work on this matter.

The final case (15) in this group involved a female barrister from outside London who was of less than 10 years call. This was more similar to the cases where mothers were represented. It had been on going for 18 months and resulted in a care order at this hearing. There had been no problems with the papers. The final fee was expected to be between £6,500 and £8,000.

(iii) Representing Other Family Members (2 Cases)

Acting for parents when a finding of fact is sought can involve work which comes closer to criminal trial procedures than is usual in family cases. In the first case (20) the female barrister of 18 years call, working in London, represented a young couple concerning a finding of fact about a non-accidental injury to their child. The papers had arrived two days before the hearing and needed to be 'sorted out'. Counsel had acted for the local authority against this solicitor in previous cases, but had not previously been instructed by the practice. The solicitors had sought her out because they had seen her in action for the local authority. A finding was made against the father, but the risk to the child was thought to be manageable and counsel expected to be involved at pre-hearing review and disposal hearings. The fee for this hearing was the standard FGFS rate with two Special Issue Payment (SIP) uplifts because there were more than two parties, experts were used, and there were allegations of significant harm to the child. Payment was expected within three months, but this barrister left the chasing to her billing clerk.

A far less contentious case (23) was that described by a male barrister of 10 years call, working in London, who acted for a grandmother whose daughter had died. She was seeking a residence order for her grandchildren. The hearing was for final directions in the County Court, and the local authority withdrew from the case. Counsel's clerk would bill the LSC directly, which he thought to be an improvement on the days when counsel had to wait for the solicitor to be paid by the LSC before counsel could be paid.

(iv) Representing the Local Authority (2 Cases)

Working for the local authority involved similarly difficult sets of circumstances, but the way the work was organised was more struc- tured, reflecting the increasing specialisation of local authorities and sets of chambers in this field. A London-based barrister of 20 years call described his most recent hearing (35) as very unusual; in fact the most difficult he had ever done. The papers had arrived 'in dribs and drabs' over nine months, and the case was expected to go to a final hearing. The hearing described was a finding of fact, in a case of alleged gross sexual abuse. This part of the case took 18 days and the clerks had agreed fees in blocks. The local authority pays counsel direct, and his fee is £150 per hour. But a consortium of six local authorities have banded together to improve their bargaining capacity, and ask for competitive tendering by chambers. In this counsel's view, public law was becoming increasingly specialised, and less likely to be carried out by high street firms. The public law QCs were described as having to go out on circuit.

The other case (14), in which a junior barrister acted for the local authority, was a final hearing where orders were made. The barrister was based outside London. He was the first counsel on the case, had received papers at the allocation hearing, and also attended a professionals' meeting. He expected payment within two months.

(v) Representing the Guardian *ad Litem* (2 Cases)

Case (1) was a care proceedings final hearing in the High Court, listed for three days. Our respondent, of 15 years call and from outside London, was the fourth barrister to work on it. He had been booked in January six months ahead of a hearing listed for June. Professionals and experts had met in February and a pre-hearing review had been held in May. There were 1,000 pages of documents, of which 10 per cent were paginated, and final papers were received late on a Thursday afternoon for a Monday hearing. In all, he had spent five full days in court and 50 hours doing preparatory work. The expected payment was £5,000, under the FGFS with uplifts (SIPs) for a foreign expert, and very significant harm. The barrister estimated his hourly rate (which included extensive input over weekends and at other unsocial hours) at £55.

In the second such case (12), the London-based female QC was publicly funded. The papers had arrived a month early and in good order. She had held two conferences with the guardian and the solicitor. The clerk had not yet billed, as the case was a high-cost case falling outside the FGFS. Payment was expected in six months. Given the complexity of the family circumstances (a nine-day hearing and nine children), the process appeared to work efficiently.

III. Private Law Children Cases (8 Cases)

10 barristers were interviewed about cases which included a private law matter involving children, but two of these cases are dealt with elsewhere, as one progressed to become a care case and has been included in the preceding section, and another was primarily a finance case, and will be included in the ancillary relief section. Of the three men and five women barristers doing private law children work, one man was based in London, one outside London but with a London base, and one outside London without a London base. Of the women, one was from London, one outside but with a London base, and three were from outside London. The non-London barristers were from Southampton, Birmingham, Preston, Manchester, Taunton and Oxford.

There were no QCs doing private law children cases, but two male and one female senior juniors had been called in the 1970s, three women in the 1990s, and one man and one woman after 2000. There was no obvious relationship between year of call and location but the women were younger. The implication may be that young men entering the profession are not drawn to private law children work. As one barrister said about publicly-funded private law work: 'They've got us over a barrel'. Another described the work as a duty, and had in fact retrained from solicitor to barrister in order to be able to carry on doing legal aid work when the firm withdrew from the publicly-funded sector. However, we may note that the LSC Strategy Paper[4] found that, in 2005–06, 40 per cent of publicly-funded private law cases still used counsel, at an average cost of £1,368.

The private law children cases were very different from the stereotypical image of irresponsible parents arguing about which day is most convenient for a visit, or even about continuing a marital dispute by arguing about the children. Even in this small sample we were told about an abduction to the Indian subcontinent, an application to prohibit vexatious litigation, child sexual abuse, and violence. These are serious cases, where legal representation matters.

A. Range of Cases

Four of our barristers were acting for mothers and four for fathers. But, as we have also suggested in the public law cases, the range of

---

[4] See above n 2.

circumstances and matters dealt with was extensive. Of the barristers acting for the mothers, there was one relatively straightforward 'specific issues' case (4), but there were also cases of abuse (2), of abduction (24), and of a mother seeking to establish contact not having seen her child for over four years (37). Where fathers were represented, the cases ranged from one fairly straightforward example of contact problems (13) to a father concerned about the baby's safety in view of the mother's mental health (28), a father trying to locate his children abroad (25), and one vexatious litigant (21).

(i) Parental Differences (2 Cases)

The 'specific issues' case (4) was concerned with future plans for the children's education. The woman barrister of 15 years call was based outside London. She described the solicitor's preparation of papers as 'exemplary'. She billed on the basis of an estimation of seven hours for a day in court, and every hour in court required an hour of preparation. Actual expenses were not charged to the client, but set against tax. Travelling time was not charged for local journeys, but for long distances would be charged at half her usual rate. It was possible that she would work on another case while travelling, and if so, this might be charged at the full rate of £150 to £200 per hour. Her clerk works on an hourly basis for billing. In this case she had given advice in May (a three hours and 10 minutes telephone conference). Preparation time was seven hours and 15 minutes, and a conference was held at court for one hour and 45 minutes. The hearing took two hours and 45 minutes, and drafting the order took a further 45 minutes. The fee was £2,000 for 12 hours and 30 minutes, that is, under £170 an hour.

In the contact case, which settled (13), a woman barrister of less than 10 years call had represented a father who was seeking contact. She had been involved with the case for over a year, and it had involved several directions hearings and a finding of fact. She regularly worked with the instructing solicitor who had prepared the papers well. At this final hearing the case had settled, though subject to a review. There had been 'a lot of work', with two conferences before the hearing as well as conferences at court. Her fee would be about £1,000, including a number of SIPs, to be met by the LSC. As to timing of payment, she said: 'Your guess is as good as mine'.

(ii) Cases Involving Welfare Issues (6 Cases)

Six further cases might be characterised as involving welfare rather than merely parental differences.

Case (25) was a directions hearing initiated by a father who wished to locate his child in another jurisdiction. The papers had been sent by the instructing solicitor in good order and in good time and the child had been located. For four hours work, the publicly-funded fee was £120, with an uplift of £60 in recognition of the foreign element. The London-based woman barrister (called in 1993) did not expect to receive payment for six to eight months.

Case (28) raised issues about the safety of a 12-month-old baby whose mother had a history of mental illness. The father sought residence. His barrister was a senior junior, based in the north, called before 1980, who did not usually do this kind of work but was covering for another counsel. As it was in the High Court, it carried a higher fee. He described the solicitor's preparation as good, and was accustomed to working with that firm, though not necessarily with the individual solicitor. The case was publicly funded, and the fee not yet known. There was a four-day final hearing. The judge made an order for shared residence, which increased the father's time with the child from two days (involving four journeys of 20 miles each way) to four days. This was not set in stone, but was likely to stand until the child began school, when five days might be more suitable. Payment was not expected for another six to nine months, and would be on a graduated fee basis for 38 hours preparation, four days in court, SIPs for experts and special preparation and one conference for each hearing day.

The third of these cases (37) involved representation by a young female barrister (called after 2000, and working outside London) of a mother who had been seeking staying contact with her child for over four years. The in-court conciliation appointment was successful in establishing a plan for staying contact, and the brief fee was £250 under the FGFS, to be paid by the LSC.

The final three 'welfare' cases were of a significantly higher level of seriousness. In case (2) the barrister represented a mother who sought a finding of fact that her husband had abused the two children, who were both under five. She was resisting his application for unsupervised contact. The barrister was relatively junior (less than 10 years call) and based in London. He had been involved in two directions hearings, and a final hearing was set down for two days in June. The total time spent on preparation was 25.5 hours, and time spent in court, including waiting and negotiating, was also 25.5 hours. There were also two 2-hour conferences with the client in chambers. The legal aid remuneration was £3,250, or £40 per hour, with special uplift payments for an extra two hours because of the difficulty of the case. The barrister described how, in private work, the clerk negotiates a price which might go up to £100 per hour, depending on the means of the client, but it could also be affected by whether the chambers wished to work again with a particular solicitor.

Counsel representing a paternal grandmother told of her High Court case (24) where her client's application for contact was resisted by the mother who had been abducted to the Indian subcontinent and had recently returned to this country after some years to be reunited with her children. The mother's former husband and his mother, counsel's client, had subsequently served custodial sentences. The case was publicly funded under the FGFS.

Finally (21) we heard from counsel acting for a vexatious litigant who was applying for residence and contact in a long and difficult case, in which the children had been moved around the country. The father would find them, and send inappropriate gifts, breaching the terms of the earlier orders. After the hearing the solicitors, with whom this barrister worked closely and regularly, sent the father a letter reminding him of the terms of his order and telling him that the police would be informed if he was in breach. The woman barrister in this case had been called in the early 1990s. There were volumes of bundles from previous proceedings, which she estimated involved 10 hours preparation for this hearing. There had been a great deal of preparation for this hearing, a conference with the client, and a professional meeting with all the lawyers involved to draft letters to the child and adult psychiatrists. Legal aid had been withdrawn shortly before the hearing, so the barrister had agreed to act at legal aid rates. Then it transpired that the case could be legally aided, so she had now sent in her SIPs form, reflecting the uplifts to be paid with respect to the complexity of the case, for the judge to sign. For her brief fee she would earn £220.30 plus VAT, £267 plus VAT, and £495 plus VAT. This barrister had formerly worked as a solicitor, but her firm had been discussing discontinuing legally aided work, so she had retrained in order to be able to continue. In her view there are very few people doing childcare work in her region, as it is uneconomical, hard, emotionally draining and difficult, but it as an area of law in which 'people must be represented and the but it as an area of law in which 'people must be represented and the government is unwilling to pay'. She seemed to consider children work as a single entity, making little distinction between private and public law matters.

These findings raise questions about the continuing need for accessible legal advice and representation in private as well as public law matters, and perhaps also for re-visiting the procedural distinction between public and private law in child-related matters, so long after they were brought together in the Children Act 1989. Numbers are small, but may be indicative of the concerns expressed by the bar, that young barristers are not interested in taking on this kind of work (Table 1).

Table 1 Summary table of counsel in children cases

Date of call	1970s	1980s	1990s	After 2000
Public Law 14 counsel (7 women, 2 QCs, 12 LSC funded)	2	5	5	2
Private Law 8 counsel (5 women, no QCs, 6 LSC funded)	3	0	3	2

IV. Financial Cases (14 Cases)

We now turn to cases which dealt with financial and property matters. We have information about 14 such cases, including one about inheritance.

Despite the small numbers in the sample, we record the age, gender and geographical profile of barristers who did these cases, in order to see whether there might be any differences from the profile of those doing children work (Table 2). Seven worked from London and eight from outside. There were three publicly-funded cases. It is not appropriate to calculate percentages for these low numbers, but it may be that barristers taking children cases are more likely to have a base outside London, and show a broader age range than those accepting financial cases, where there was only one barrister called after 2000 in our sample.

Table 2 Summary table of counsel in financial cases

	Date of call			
	1970s	1980	1990s	After 2000
Men	1	2	5	0
Women	2	2	1	1

A. Range of Cases

Of the 14 barristers who reported financial cases to us, two described final hearings, and one a successful Financial Dispute Resolution hearing which would obviate the need for a final hearing. Six counsel described their involvement at an earlier stage in the case in directions hearings, some of which it had been thought might become Financial Dispute Resolution (FDR) hearings but had failed to reach that stage and remained as directions hearings. There were also three first directions hearings, one about maintenance only, and finally two rather unusual cases, one of which did not go to court at all and one outlying case of adult children questioning an inheritance.

(i) Final Hearings (2 Cases)

We begin with the most complex procedures, the two final hearings. The first (5) was long running, but counsel described to us how the solicitors had pushed forward to a final hearing when the female barrister of 20 years call had expected more negotiation to follow after the FDR hearing. Counsel was for the wife. The case was adjourned for a written judgment, not yet received. It was a FGFS case, so the barrister expected to be paid fairly soon but said: 'It won't be very much money'. The second final hearing (6) had been set for three days and concerned variation of maintenance and the capitalisation thereof. There had been three interlocutory hearings of three to four hours each, two conferences with the client and solicitors over the two years, but no QC had been involved. The case did not settle and ran its three days, even requiring an additional half-day. The other side was expected to appeal. The final hearing brief fee with refreshers was approximately £8,000, with another £8–10,000 for the other four hearings and conferences. There was no public funding in this case on either side.

(ii) Financial Dispute Resolution (FDR) (1 Case)

It is always hoped that a final hearing may not be needed if a successful FDR is held at which the parties, having disclosed their assets and liabilities, meet before a judge and put forward their arguments. The judge does not adjudicate, but advises them of the likely outcome of any final hearing if they are unable to agree at this stage, and strongly advises them to avoid further conflict and expense by coming to settlement.

One of our respondents described a successful FDR hearing (32). He had received the papers two days before the hearing date. No conference was held but there was a telephone conversation with the solicitor, which the barrister liked to have on the day the papers arrived. The matter settled on the day. It was the end of the case, but the barrister, called 15 years ago and working out of London, did then draft the order. He had left heads of agreement with the court, so he was able to pass them to the judge through the door as his opponent had left and it was late in the day. The court had an emailing service, so he emailed his minutes through to the court. The fee was £800 and would be met within a couple of months. There was no public funding.

(iii) Directions Hearings Which Failed to Convert to FDR (6 Cases)

Six cases were at the stage of possibly achieving an FDR, but if the parties were not ready they would revert to being a directions hearing. In case (7) the male barrister, London based and called in the 1980s, had represented the husband at a first directions appointment. The papers had been received two weeks before the hearing, allowing for six or seven hours preparation. But the barrister described the time available for the conference as inadequate, the meeting being set for 11 am and the hearing for 2 pm. The time was taken up in heavily amending the financial questionnaires from both parties. The hearing, which was set down for 30 minutes but in fact lasted an hour, failed to achieve settlement, even though some directions had been agreed in advance between counsel. This barrister expects to take the case forward to an FDR in November. The brief fee for this part of the case was £1,650 (not publicly funded) and the barrister expected prompt payment.

In case (8) the brief had been received seven days before the hearing for directions. Counsel (of over 20 years call) had been involved with the family at an earlier stage when there were Children Act issues. The case had failed to settle, and directions were given and the case listed for

FDR. The fee (not publicly funded) was £1,200 including the conference before the hearing, and payment was expected within about three months.

In case (26) the barrister (male, out of London, called in 1972) hoped that the hearing would be would be an FDR, but the parties were unable to agree sufficiently for this to take place. The papers had arrived over the weekend, in reasonable order. Directions were given for an FDR to be held in four months time. The brief fee was £750 plus VAT. Including travel time, the barrister had been engaged for four and a half hours (£83 per hour). The two-hour conference was billed separately at £150. Payment was expected within two weeks, as the client 'wanted to pay as he went along, and the solicitors like to get the money in'. There was no public funding. Case (27) was a first directions hearing for an application for maintenance pending suit. The papers had arrived in good time, with some deficiencies attributable to the client, not the solicitor. The case was listed for an FDR re the substantive application. The brief fee of £1500 was expected to be paid promptly.

In case (30) the papers had arrived two weeks before the hearing, and were updated for the hearing. The female barrister (called over 20 years ago, working outside London) had prepared a position document and draft order for the hearing. There was one conference, and the hearing was set down as a first directions appointment hearing or FDR. There was dispute over disclosure, so negotiations were limited and there was no settlement. The case was subsequently listed for a date the barrister could not attend, and the barrister insisted that it was very unusual for her to return a case, as she would generally see a case through to final hearing. She stressed that she never double booked, and did her own clerking. The brief fee was £1,750. In the final possible FDR case, (36) the female barrister, called after 2000, from out of London, represented the husband. She had been briefed at the last minute to respond to a request to vary a maintenance order made by consent some two years earlier and found that she would have to ask for an adjournment as her client has not prepared his financial statement (Form E). The brief fee was £400 for 45 minutes in court, neither party attending.

(iv) First Directions Appointments (3 cases)

Case (9) was a first directions hearing in a County Court with a request for maintenance pending suit. There was no legal aid. Papers had arrived two weeks earlier in good order, and the male barrister (from London, called in 1995) had worked with the instructing solicitor previously. The hearing was set for 30 minutes and completed to time, and an order for maintenance was made, together with costs and a penal notice. The brief fee was £750 and would be paid shortly. The second case (17) was primarily concerned with ancillary relief. It involved business premises and a flat, but there had also been proceedings about contact. The barrister was publicly funded, and particularly interested in the case as it involved a novel point of law concerning the alleged influence over the mother of the father's family who had effectively kept her and the child, then a baby, for five years while she was expected to work for the family business for nothing. The language and geographical issues required extra time on the case for all the legal representatives.

Case (22) concerned an application to vary periodic payments for a child. It was privately funded. The papers had arrived the Friday before the Monday hearing in reasonable order. The female barrister (called in the early 1990s) frequently worked with the instructing solicitor. There were no conferences except at court. The directions hearing resulted in a list of directions and an additional application. The barrister expected to be instructed for the next stage of the matter, which would be an FDR. The barrister was not sure of the brief fee, but expected payment within a month or two.

(v) Two Unusual Cases

The last two cases both have unusual features. Case (27) was an ancillary relief case with associated children matters. There was no public funding, and no court hearing. The barrister said he had spent many hours ('hundreds') on the case, and charged on an hourly basis. The case involved a divorce, the financial aspects of the divorce, and whether a child who had been taken into care in the course of the dispute should be returned to the parents. The outcome was that the financial aspects were settled by consent, and the child was returned to the parents. The final case (33) was a claim by an adult child under the family provision legislation, which was publicly funded. The solicitors came to see the barrister three weeks before trial, and the barrister recommended a freezing injunction as there was a risk there would be no estate left. The barrister then went before a deputy master and was granted the injunction. The trial was held 10 days later. There was a different judge and the appeal for relief was not successful. The fee was £4,000, with refreshers.

4

Financial Cases

I. Introduction

THIS AND THE following two chapters are based on the observational data derived from spending 20 days accompanying barristers of various levels of seniority as they went about their work. The barristers were chosen with the help of the FLBA to represent a wide geographical spread and the variety of public and private law cases in which the family law bar is involved. We had no questionnaires, but after explaining the nature of the research to the barrister, the barristers sometimes provided background information on the case. Sometimes the researcher discussed the case with the barrister at the end of the day, but the major task was to record the barristers' activities manually. Following the techniques developed for our earlier study of solicitors, we contacted the FLBA to explain the project, and here record our thanks to the FLBA for publishing an account of the research in *Family Affairs*, encouraging members of the Family Bar to take part in the project, and providing contacts and information on cases. From the barristers who approached us following this invitation, we selected individuals to cover a range of seniority, geographical location and type of work. We explained the project and assured the participants that all published information would be anonymised, and that all research notes would be stored separately from any identifying information. We did not attempt to tape record, as this would have been impracticable on account of the number of individuals involved during a day in court. However full notes were taken, and later transcribed. The data were then analysed using the Framework technique developed by the National Centre for Social Research, (NATCEN), whereby the researchers familiarise themselves with the transcribed data and identify emerging issues to inform the development of a theoretical framework.

There are of course limitations associated with all methodologies. Our sample is not nationally 'representative' of the family law bar. But it provides examples of the range of work carried out by those involved. Qualitative research cannot say what proportion of the total population of lawyers behaves in a specified way. But it can build up a picture of the ways in which lawyers work. The lack of any similar empirical study of the profession made it impossible to begin in any other way. Without a description of the tasks undertaken, skills employed, goals aimed at, and constraints experienced, we could not develop sensible questions for the larger scale quantitative work which we hope will follow.

This chapter will describe the work done by barristers of various levels of seniority in six financial cases arising from separation and divorce. Three of the cases (two of which involved QCs on both sides as well as senior juniors) are what are generally termed 'big money' cases, involving assets of many millions of pounds with complex arrangements including trusts, tax management, venture capitalism, etc. A fourth case was a medium money matter, which tried to stretch one middle-class income to cover two households. The other two cases were more concerned with coping with lack of money than its allocation, and involved mortgage foreclosure, benefit entitlement and bankruptcy proceedings. Both of the 'no money' cases were publicly funded. One was taken by a member of one of the specialist chambers who also did 'big money' cases, the other by a young barrister from provincial chambers who described his practice as the 'nightmare end of the family bar'.

This cross-cutting of areas of work by experience and status of counsel confirmed our view that we should group our material according to case type rather than by seniority or location of counsel. We did indeed see the same kinds of tasks being done and the same specialised skills being used by all counsel doing financial work. Clearly knowledge of law and procedure is a primary requirement. The aim of this study, however, is not to discuss, or even to evaluate, the legal framework. Rather, it is to describe the variety of skills employed by barristers, ranging from the techniques of accountancy and audit, use of local knowledge (of the court, opposing counsel and judiciary, of schools and housing markets) to people management in interaction with clients, instructing solicitors, counsel, judiciary and court staff, containing elements of counselling, negotiation and, of course, advocacy.

In the accounts which follow in this and the subsequent two chapters, names, where used, are fictitious, and we have altered various incidental 'facts' to prevent the actual case from being identified. As a further means to prevent identification, we will only say that the data were collected at some time after January 2004.

II.   George and the 'World Businessman'

George is a 'senior' junior, specialising in privately-funded ancillary relief work, in specialist London chambers. He described himself as perhaps more of a team player than some of his colleagues, seeing less of a sharp dividing line between his work and that of the instructing solicitor. An example was his willingness to help put together the papers in a case. On this Wednesday morning he arrived in chambers at 8 am. He checked with the clerks whether documents on another case had arrived. There were four clerks with a bank of computers, busy negotiating fees, filling diaries, protecting counsel from phone calls, and finding out which judge was sitting where. George was to meet with the female QC leading him at 8.30. He had prepared the note for the judge the previous Monday, and revised the available figures as advised by the instructing solicitor. The client was expected with the solicitor at 10 am for a conference preceding the Financial Dispute Resolution hearing (FDR) set down for 3 pm. In such cases both sides are asked to make full financial disclosure and set out their proposals for a financial settlement before the hearing. The judge will be actively involved in trying to help them reach settlement by giving them an idea of the kind of outcome which could be expected in a final adjudicative hearing. The judge can make a consent order, or set down the case for a final hearing, which must be before another member of the judiciary.

The client was a wealthy venture capitalist whose wife had petitioned for divorce three years earlier. The three children were living with her, and the client had accepted responsibility for their expenses. The matters at issue were the ratio for the division of the assets, and the date at which these assets were to be evaluated. The client was offering 50 per cent of those assets which had been invested before separation but not yet realised. The wife sought 40 per cent of the present assets. There was considerable uncertainty in the papers about precise figures. The client was seeking agreement about the principle by which the assets would be divided. The other side sought precise figures. On the Friday the client had made an offer to provide a fair resolution on a clean break basis. If this was not accepted at the FDR, there would need to be a final hearing of three or four days some months later. Costs already exceeded £70,000, but this was not a major concern for the client.

George explained to the researcher something of his techniques for client management. 'I say to them "this is a blip in your life … it may last six months but life goes on … There is a lot of life to be lived"'. He went in to meet the QC. The meeting began with discussion about client management tactics. The QC said: 'We'll let him run the meeting … give him the power here and then guide him towards settlement'. He and George together set up the elegant meeting room. The QC wanted the client far away from her at the head of the table. George wanted to be close and 'tactile', but was overruled. The two counsel talked through the psychology of the parties. 'How does she deal with this person? … she will get the money but we don't know when … she could just wait … does she need the hassle? His income is well concealed'.

The client and the instructing solicitor arrived at 10.30. Coffee was brought in and the female solicitor served it. The client was charming. He deferentially asked about the court appearance, whether he should wear a tie, and what would happen. This was the QC's cue to offer expert insider knowledge about the idiosyncrasies of the judge, and explain that an order cannot be imposed, although if the client agrees to an order, it may be binding even if he changes his mind. She quoted a recent House of Lords case. She explained that the judge was there to listen to the parties, to identify points of difficulty, and to broker a settlement and indicate the cost of going to trial.

> The client asks whether everything is without prejudice. The QC says 'yes, except for threats', and 'if you declare X and you have Y, that is privileged but the other side would use it'. She says bluntly that she is pessimistic about reaching agreement. The client puts forward multiple justifications for his position but the QC maintains that, even if the wife were willing to agree to the client's suggestions, her legal representatives have a professional duty to protect her interests and would seek firm figures before accepting any proposals. The client maintains that the outcomes of his business activities are like future share prices and cannot be quantified. It emerges that he has had a row with the solicitor on this point the Friday before. The QC uses language with delicacy to press her point: 'You put it persuasively … but may we refine your argument'. Figures are discussed. 'Let's break it down'. The QC continues to press the client on tax and real amounts, and is supported by the solicitor who adds in further figures, and identifies an item of double counting. By 11 am the QC appears slightly flustered by the figures, while the client has become calmer. The QC: 'We need a new schedule … the figures change all the time … pre and post tax … this figure is an illusion. We need numbers'. The client: 'My attempt is to get them to think about it conceptually, then we can get to figures, what do you

think?' The QC: 'It depends on the personalities; she may be wanting clarity, to get on with her life, *or* she might want her day in court and your head on a plate'. She feels hampered by having 'no conversation with the other side' on which to base negotiation.

At this point, 12 noon, a clerk brought in the note from the other side and the meeting closed to allow the legal representatives to withdraw and examine it, and for the client to make further phone calls. The note highlighted the issue of distinguishing between present assets and income which will not be available for some years to come, and it appeared to the QC that the wife was looking for a share of income. She rapidly checked recent cases on her computer. George then identified a problem about a possible failure by the client to disclose a letter, which he thought would have to be put to the client. The QC was reluctant, but George said: 'We have to come clean'. The solicitor and George threw in further facts and cases, while the QC looked rather desperately for a line of argument. The clock was running. The QC was concerned about possible criticism from the other side. These included members of neighbouring chambers, so her anxiety about criticism from that quarter revealed an interesting form of professional control. At 1.30 the QC was writing her notes for court, over sandwiches. At 1.40 a convey-ancing issue arose with respect to the sale of one of the client's properties. It was dealt with. The disclosure issue was put to the client, who responded: 'Do I *have* to produce the letter?' 'Yes' replied the QC firmly.

At 2 pm a clerk wheeled the 32 lever arch files over to court. The QC followed, with the client, keeping him calm, together with George and the solicitor, chatting about other cases. Parties are invited to attend an hour or so before an FDR so as to give time for negotiation. When we arrived, the QC found a conference room, and told the other side where they were. She then became busy re-numbering the pages in her documents as the court bundle had different pagination. She said: 'We don't want to appear desperate to settle ... if they haven't appeared by 2.45 we will knock on their door'. The client began biting his nails. At 2.40 the other side knocked.

They say they can't negotiate without figures. It is 15 minutes before they are due before the judge. The four lawyers move into the corridor and rapid exchanges take place. The other side brings up a child-related issue as a bargaining device. It is rejected. They ask for an affidavit to be produced quickly containing all they know with supporting documents, because 'you're not playing fair'. The QC replies that this is an unfair comment, and asks the other side for a similar affidavit, to be followed by a round table meeting. The other side joke about block-buster affidavits. Both agree they cannot settle in the FDR, but can agree directions. The juniors from both sides write these out for the judge, by hand, leaning on the wall in the corridor.

They returned to the client in the conference room. The QC explained that she understood his view that the wife was prepared to deal but her lawyers would not let her. They insisted on numbers, and were wary about any settlement without documents. The client maintained that he did not know and could not tell what the net assets were, so he could only talk about principles.

In court the atmosphere was formal. The judge, flanked by assistants, sat on a dais, with QCs in front and clients, solicitors and juniors behind. Apparently QCs traditionally sit one space in from the gangway and two spaces apart so that they have equal eye contact with the judge. Solicitors sit behind with the client. The QC read out the agreed directions. The other side asked the judge if he had read their note. The judge replied that he had received it at 2 pm and would read it now. The QC said that all the questions were answered months ago, and there had been no queries or complaint until today. The judge made the order as requested and asked for the bundles to be taken away.

At 3.30, back in the conference room, the QC explained to the client that he must produce an affidavit. The client replied that he was still reluctant to do that, as the figures would change and the position was complex. 'The more information I give them the more confused they'll get'. The QC replied: 'You can explain in baby language', adding that there was some professional 'back saving' on the part of the other side. She would cut through and settle if she could. The QC said: 'Please set out the history of your relationship: chronology, financial timetable, different kinds of assets. If the other side are better informed they may settle. If not, it will act as evidence if we go to trial'. The child-related issue was raised again (without any mention of the best interests of the child) and was dealt with constructively by George. The group returned to chambers at 4.50. It was agreed that George and the solicitor would take the matter forward.

In this case counsel had not expected to settle. They were dealing with a powerful and articulate client who had a firm view and would not be persuaded of the need to meet the other side's demands for a figure to negotiate around. Despite their best efforts at flattery, reason, and use of legal precedent, this 'World Businessman' would not be persuaded. Even the argument of potentially increased costs did not sway him. Although the divorce did not seem to be particularly acrimonious, this client would not be persuaded. Negotiation failed, but it was at the stage of negotiation with the client rather than with the other side. Given the stormy history of the client's relationship with his solicitor, the case demonstrated that cases do not necessarily come to court because of their complexity, but can do so because of the client's certainty in his position and refusal to take advice. The fees were £7,500 for the QC, and £3,750 to Junior Counsel.

III. Caroline and the Novelist

Caroline was being led by a QC, who had been called in after the first hearing because of the amounts of money at stake, and the client was accompanied by his solicitor. The attention given to how the room in chambers was set up was again apparent. While waiting for the client there were pleasantries between the members of chambers about other international cases, about dinner parties, and other tension-relieving devices. This case was a somewhat unusual set of circumstances, though the nature of the work is such that counsel rarely see 'usual' circumstances. The husband was seeking ancillary relief from his former wife. The couple were not high earners. Both were writers, but there was substantial capital of over £1 million derived from the wife's family. In the discussion prior to the meeting, the QC (who had represented husbands in a number of similar cases recently) remarked that any court would 'expect him to get off his financial backside ... I will give him the advice that courts discriminate against husbands who claim against their wives'. The couple had always shared care of their children and planned to go on doing so. There was no disagreement over this. They met frequently to talk about the children and were seeing a counsellor to help them to manage this.

Caroline explained that the husband was seeking enough money to house himself in such a way that there would not be too great a disparity between the children's two homes. The two barristers discussed the progress of the case, procedural tactics and problems that had arisen at the First Appointment, when the solicitors from the other side had been 'hyper', objecting to 90 per cent of their questions. There was discussion about whether they should go to the High Court. Caroline asked: 'Where will we do better re future wealth?' The QC said it would be better to leave it with a District Judge. Caroline said: 'But if we're making big arguments, a DJ will be mean and frightened'. Then they turned to previous relevant cases, house prices in the area, how judges viewed husbands and wives in this kind of situation, and how the FDR had been handled. The QC asked about the judge who had presided over the FDR: 'Is she an applicant's DJ or a wife's DJ?' Caroline answered: 'the wife … she's so capricious'. At 3 pm the client and his solicitor arrived. He seemed calm and a rather gentle soul. The QC opened the meeting by sounding aggressive about the wife: 'We have her schedule of assets … she's been spending money'. The client replied quietly that he wasn't good with numbers; he would listen and try to help, to clarify. He could explain her expenditure as related to house sales and moves. 'She's not a spender, not extravagant'.

At this stage, rather than being encouraged to develop the argument about the wife's spending, the QC was being reined back by the client, and had to ask: 'If I say in my summary that she doesn't have to worry about money, that she is a wealthy lady, is that OK?' As with the 'World Businessman', there was gap between the legal framing of the matter and the way the client saw things. The client was making a claim against his former wife, but was reluctant to paint the kind of picture about the wife that would be necessary if a judge were to be persuaded to accept the claim. The client brought the discussion back from his wife's assets and spending to what mattered to him, which was 'how I live with the kids'. He was concerned that they should be able to enjoy their time with him without feeling that the lifestyle was too different from when they were with their mother. They should live in a reasonable place and there should be a fund to enable him to take them on holidays. He wanted to keep his house. He thought the legal arguments about his need to achieve financial independence were hopeless.

> The QC says there will be issues over keeping the house. He will be expected to sell and buy somewhere cheaper, but he can ask for some maintenance. The solicitor advises a lump sum. The client says: 'It would just go into some account to pay for holidays'. The lawyers are talking about 'grounds to depart from equality … inheritance extraneous to the marriage … life expectancies … reasonable needs … clean break … our offer . . . you need seed corn capital while you get a job unless she accepts'. The client breaks in: 'I find the whole money thing horrendous. I'm not thinking about myself'. The lawyers throw in more and more detailed figures, and complex housing moves. The client breaks in again, surprising them by saying: 'But that's less than is on offer when I am talking to Sue'. Caroline says: 'But we're lawyers … they (her counsel) have to advise her … if she says "Ok", then her solicitors won't stop her but they will tell her this is not what a court would order'. The solicitor

suggests drawing the other side out. The QC moves closer to the client's position, but seems taken aback by the intervention. He says: 'We'll try for the house. Don't go and talk to Sue. We don't want them writing back saying you're badgering her. If she's decent about it she'll admit she discussed it'. The client says: 'She's decent. She accepts my behaviour (depression). I've forgiven her the thing (a new relationship)'. The QC, now taking on board the client's position, says: 'If we write now and they accept (note, 'they' not 'she'), there is no need to go to court ... she has no more appetite for proceedings than you do'.

The lawyers revert to aggressive-sounding technical discussion about who has the Child Benefit Book, who might claim Child Support etc. The client: 'This is not what I wanted to hear. I thought it would be something to say "there is this massive amount of money", but they could force me to move house. It's madness'. The QC responds, moving even closer towards the client's position: 'The law says she must make the first offer, but her solicitors could write and be mean. There is no reason why you shouldn't talk to her if we cut out the solicitors. Talk to her, don't mention us, and if you get nowhere the solicitor should write the letter as we discussed. If you can agree, so much the better'. The client says: 'I'm grateful to you for what you've done, to see where we are. My understanding is that I shall speak to her. I have moved a long way for her'. Caroline remarks that what a rational human being thinks is fair is not necessarily what a court with rules will say, so it would be fine if the client talks to her. The client: 'We do talk. When we sit down tomorrow, I'm there for the kids'. The QC advises, to protect himself and the client: 'A negotiation between the two of you may well be the best way. The best thing to say if she asks what your lawyers said is "you wouldn't expect to tell me what your lawyers said"'. The client replies: 'I will build up my discussion with her, say I've been going through the papers. The house is non-negotiable. As for the rest, I would like a pot for the kids we can both use maybe'.

The meeting ended. The lawyers were pessimistic about the outcome, but heard later that the couple had agreed. This client had benefited from learning how a court might react to the kind of claim he was making, and this convinced him that the best way to secure what he wanted was to negotiate directly. The lawyers supported him in this, and advised on the best way to do this while protecting his own position.

IV. Louise and the Surprise Ending

In the third case involving substantial assets, Louise, a senior junior in London chambers, represented a wife who was seeking an attachment of earnings order, as her former husband had failed to pay maintenance for four months. He was seeking a reduction in the order. The case was set down as a 'floater' (that is, with no fixed time for the hearing) in the Principal Registry of the Family Division for that day. Louise explained to her client, who was with her solicitor, that the court could only deal with the matter in a summary way today, but that if her former husband sought a reduction, then according to a recent case he needed to demonstrate that his circumstances had changed. So far no such evidence had been produced. The husband claimed that his firm had agreed to pay the mortgage on his new flat, but that while work was being done there, he was living in a hotel and having to pay two sets of housing costs. But there was no evidence of hotel bills.

After a brief conference, they moved over to the court. Louise was delighted to find that the other side did not have counsel, only a solicitor who she thought was no match for her! Everyone was tense, but settled down on finding a room. The client was distressed. She was in her late 40s and had not worked during the nine-year marriage. She had a son from a previous relationship who was still in full-time education at an agricultural college. She said she had no money, and no earnings. Louise's strategy was to investigate further into the husband's expenses and assets. 'We could seek information from third parties … a Swiss bank', but then she reminded the client that 'this is a costly exercise, and might produce nothing. He may have boxed himself into a corner by refusing bank statements early on and now can't lose face'. The client anxiously produced more and more detail on his spending and assets. She was well acquainted with his activities, which included international travel and partying. But Louise rested on the argument that he had produced no evidence of his hotel or any other expenses. But then the client revealed that she had phoned the hotel a few days ago and they said he was staying there. Louise's best argument suddenly looked very vulnerable.

She tried to stay calm and appear in control, maintaining that there was still no evidence, such as hotel bills, and he could not expect the benefit of the doubt. The young solicitor was concerned that the whole hour for the hearing would be used up by his request for variation, and there would be no time for the client's request for attachment of earnings. Louise fell back on hoping that 'we will get an experienced full-time judge. We're floating … we don't know which judge'. There were further discussions about other international properties and accounts. It was really just filling in the time and keeping the client calm. Then on looking through credit card statements, the client found a hotel bill. Louise's main argument was destroyed.

> The barrister resorts to saying: 'The judge can say he just can't draw up a list of his expenses and put you at the bottom ... he's going to look *so bad* at the final hearing'. She tries to lower the tension. The client talks about her court demeanour. 'I'm trying to be less arrogant ... judges don't like it ... he's arrogant ... can we ask for costs?' Louise tells the researcher that she hates hanging around as a floater. They may have to wait till 4 30 pm. The client needs to be soothed. She has to stay and put in the time but only gets compensated for delay at legal aid rates. We go over to court at 11.15 and find a room. The solicitor suggests checking the valuation of the flat, and calls the estate agent. The agent sends pictures directly from the flat showing used wine glasses, unmade beds and other clear evidence that it is being lived in. Louise is vastly relieved. She speaks to the solicitor representing the husband and asks for details of payments for the flat. He says they did not accept that the liabilities for the flat are theirs, but are the company's and therefore they have no information on how payments were made. Louise is jubilant. There can be no evidence of double housing costs, and no other change of circumstance has been argued. She says that she will ask for bank statements on penal notice within seven days. The husband's solicitor tells her that his client was afraid of the Revenue. Louise and her solicitor agreed that the solicitor for the husband was indeed a 'numpty', as predicted, and they expect to win.

It was an exciting morning, with evidence gathering still ongoing in the manner of a criminal trial rather than an ancillary relief hearing. The experienced client showed surprising attention to detail, finding points missed by her lawyers. But Louise's faith in the ineptness of the other side was in the event justified. A tense wait followed. Louise retreated back to chambers at lunchtime, leaving the client with the solicitor. She checked a point of law on foreign evidence with a colleague, but essentially needed a break from the confines of the conference room with the anxious client, with whom she had been closeted since 10 am. The parties waited until 4.30 pm, when to Louise's dismay the district judge found for the husband!

V. Charles and the Failing Small Businessman

In this out-of-London case, Charles was a junior from a specialist London chambers, and claimed to be embarrassed about taking the case. There were negative assets and a low income. The client was still in the former matrimonial home and the wife and three children under five were in local authority housing and on benefits. The client owned a flat, and had a failing small business. The wife was seeking the sale of the house and a share in the proceeds of sale. The client's resistance to the claim did not look promising.

Charles and the researcher left London at 10 am. Charles read the papers on the train. He arrived at court at 12 noon, where he met the client and a local solicitor. The volunteer coffee stall had just closed for the day. Charles was pleased to hear the judge was someone he regarded as very sensible. He found a room, and began to question the client forcefully.

'You're being assaulted from all sides, about the children, your behaviour . . . We must clarify the finances. I need your income position. Are you living hand to mouth?' The client replies that he knows his salary but not his drawings, and has bank statements. Charles looks at the papers and sees an error. He rings his clerk to fax the right document. He says: 'I can't see how you hold on to these two properties (the former matrimonial home and a rented flat)'. The client attributes his failure to earn to his unhappy situation and pressure from his wife. 'When this is over, I'll work. I've lost my job over this. It's not fair to ask for money and not let me work'. Charles asks what his income was before the proceedings. The client says he can only go by the published accounts. So the barrister asks for his estimated earnings. '£8,000 a year'. Charles says that the other side are asking for disclosure of his mortgage applications, which include details of income. The client replies that he had to estimate these for a consumer credit account. The barrister says that the other side will ask how he got a mortgage on this level of income: 'You're storing up debt. I need to know your outgoings and net income'.

The exchanges sounded like angry cross-examination, testing of evidence rather than an advocate taking instruction.

The client then begins to defend his position. 'I'm paying voluntary maintenance, more than the CSA would set based on these accounts. That's why no order for interim maintenance was made. What she's asking is ludicrous ... I couldn't focus on my work ... everything she's doing is counterproductive'. Charles asks: 'Do you want to stop this hassle? What she will want to know is what you plan to do after this is over. What income can you generate? Is this a blip or is it ruin, bankruptcy? You're saying you have to meet liabilities'. The client replies: 'You have the bank accounts, the bank doesn't lie, it's all here'. His contract is unclear. The accounts indicate an annual turnover of £60,000 and that he was to work partly in London and partly at home, but apparently he has not billed for all the days. Charles, losing patience, asks what he thought his wife wanted. 'I used to live with her and I don't know. My ultimate ruin?' The client continues, explaining how he normally finds his own contracts, but hasn't had any payments yet from the company for whom he now works. The edge goes out of the confrontation. Barrister and client begin to look together at the detailed figures. Charles explains that he is trying to establish a factual base. He goes steadily through the entire set of papers, checking income and expenditure, and though a little chaotic and complex, the picture emerges in accordance with the client's version of events. There do not seem to be any concealed assets.

The separation had been relatively non-acrimonious. There had been regular contact between them until a few months ago when the wife stopped the client's contact with the youngest child, and accused the client of substance abuse. He said that this was the event that triggered his inability to work properly. He felt isolated, wrongly accused, and unable to work, while his wife had the children, her family and friends, and should be able to go back to work after her maternity leave. 'She's grinding me into the ground. There's no money'. Charles now sounded less hostile, and accepted the financial position as stated, having tested the evidence rigorously with the client and solicitor. He moved on to consider the future.

He asks if the wife would want to move into the house. The client says that it's not an asset; it's a liability. The barrister points out that there is some equity, and asks what the client is doing with the assets. The client replies that the flat is for the children's future. The barrister asks if they can say that it would be held on trust for the children. The client says that he has often said that, but the wife wants half of it now. Charles agrees that it is not an income-generating asset, but it is still an asset. The client reveals a debt to a brother, but that his credit card debt is being paid off at a nominal rate per month. He blames his wife for upsetting his plan to sort out his finances. Charles, trying to focus the client's attention on the future and get away from the recriminations, says: 'How does that help me find an answer?' The client apologises, but says he wants to trade out of his difficulties. If the home were to be sold, he would have to pay higher mortgage interest payments on a two-bedroom place than he does now on a four-bedroom one. Anyway, 'why did she move out'? Charles, bluntly: 'Because she didn't like living with you... but if she asks to adjourn it will be a sword of Damocles. You don't want things hanging over you'. The client says he will not move out, as the mortgage would still have to be paid. When asked about housing benefit he admits that that there is an order on the house, and if one more month is unpaid, he will be repossessed. Charles asks, again: 'What if she wanted to move in?' 'She's short sighted' is the reply. The barrister comes back with one of the stock phrases: 'You need to put on long sighted glasses for her', but says they need to know what the other side wants. He admits that a lump sum would not be any use to her as she is on benefits.

Charles and the solicitor then went to meet the other side, the solicitor remarking how difficult he found the client. He had not worked on the case for some months, as bills had not been paid. Charles met the counsel for the wife, a young woman who did not believe the husband's account of his finances, and thought that there were further assets hidden away. She wanted everything sold and shared, and thought that the wife could buy on a part-ownership scheme. Charles returned to the conference room. The client still refused to consider selling.

Charles points out that the court could order him to sell. 'They couldn't', the client retorts, to which counsel responds: 'If she can convince the court that she will house herself and the children, the court may well order sale and ask why she isn't in the house now. Most cases are the other way around. She is in local authority accommodation with the three children and you stay in large property'. The solicitor, placatingly: 'We are playing devil's advocate'. Charles appeals to the client's pride: 'You have financial acumen. Until 2003 you were doing well. Take the emotion out of this, and look at this balance sheet. What would you say?' The client replies: 'Flat—neutral for the children; house ... and I should be allowed to work ... creditors are giving me time to get back on track, things can turn around. As they improve she will have more'. 'Why can't you sell and still work your way out of it?' asks the barrister. The client replies that he can't rent; he would need credit checks, but admits that he has not enquired. Charles says, firmly: 'I think you need to end these proceedings ... be free to work, no more fighting. I'm not interested in finding her a place. I'm interested in your finances. I think the house has to go. The debt is too big. You are in a four-bedroom house and she in local authority accommodation'. The client retorts that it was her choice to go. The barrister reminds him that this is 'irrelevant'. The client: 'I want her to have something, get out of local authority housing'. The solicitor, seizing the opportunity for movement, says: 'So, what would you propose, how would you raise a capital sum for her?' 'If she wants to keep her benefits I'll borrow from my brother. I want to preserve the house as an asset. I will pay more in future but want to protect my reputation by paying £3,000 now'. Charles also seizes the opportunity for movement, saying: 'You could agree to sell in 18 months if she shows she can re-house and work'. The client responds, reluctantly: 'It's a possibility ... the onus is on her to prove she can do it'.

The other side have not yet talked. The solicitor said he was 'fed up . . . in court for three hours and no negotiation from them'.

At this point Charles moved from collecting information to looking ahead. The solicitor and barrister do the figures together and decide that if the house is sold and debts repaid there would be £10,000 each. The barrister agreed that the wife would be better off with £3,000 and not selling.

> Charles now has a plan. Keep the maintenance nominal, no clean break because of the ages of the children, and agree sale when she guarantees re-housing and work. To the client: 'I don't want the lawyers to get all the money. If we walk away, you're on your own'. The client objects that it's not a commercial decision to sell now, and asks: 'How can I have contact in a one-bedroom flat?' Charles goes to the other side. He is told that they want a sale now, before debts can be charged against the house, and want to know the client's income. They don't believe he 'is going down the pan', but instead that there is a 'hidden pot'. Charles is firm: 'You won't find other capital. He will sell if the money is useful'. The other side wants all the equity. Charles urges opposing counsel to read the documents. She says she will; it would be negligent of her to just take his word. Charles asks for their proposal. Counsel says it will have to go for final hearing.

Charles came back and said he thought the other side might ask for an adjournment. At 3 pm they were called into court for the FDR. The layout was informal and the district judge authoritative but pleasant. The other side opened, claiming that there were gaps in the financial profile. Charles said that he had grave doubts about his client's solvency, and stressed that the contact issues raised had been dealt with and were not part of these proceedings. He said that the first issue was where the children would live:

> If she can use the equity for housing we will agree to sale. But we have no detail on the part-buying plan, five months after the earlier hearing. And no indication about her employment plan. On benefits, any lump sum will be wasted. We are open to negotiation about sale of the former matrimonial home, and please note that the husband has a new contract, needs his finances to calm down, and above all to stop spending money on these costs.

The District Judge pointed out the cost of a two-day hearing could be £15,000, which neither side could afford. He indicated that if this was a final hearing, his inclination would be to say 'sell and share', and questioned whether it was realistic for the wife to think of buying a part-owned home. Counsel for the wife repeated: 'She wants to buy a part-owned home'. The District Judge questioned whether this was realistic, and said he would reserve the case for final hearing.

Charles goes back to conference room with the client and explained that the judge is sympathetic to his problems. He then goes to talk to the other side. He says that he will not be taking the case further. The other counsel suggests a round table with the solicitors discussing the facts. For example, if part-buy was not possible then they could go back to a £3,000 lump sum and nominal periodic payments, with the husband taking responsibility for the debts. Charles returns. The client says: 'I don't understand'. Charles explains: 'The judge said, "stop fighting and wasting money, be realistic". He might say, "sell and repay debts, and she gets zip". But part-buy? No. But you should have an interest in anything she bought. It's jargon, but the District Judge believes you! There is no pot of gold. He listed a two-day hearing, but no one wants it. The Legal Services Commission won't fund if she can't go on. In two weeks there will be an information meeting here, with your solicitors, and you'll both have to compromise. Think about spending on your children's housing, not on lawyers. Stick to: we keep the flat and she gets a proportion of the equity in the home'.

Charles set off to London at 5 pm.

In this case both Charles and the judge were anxious to get the matter resolved with the best outcome for the children, and were trying to move the case forward. The barrister was much more active in advising the client than pressing for what the client was asking for. But, after rigorous checking, he did develop some sympathy for the client's point of view, namely, that he be allowed to trade out of his financial predicament, keep the properties in order to live in the home and enable the children to have staying contact with him, and to keep the flat to pass on to his children. The client argued that if the house were sold he would have to find somewhere else to live. But Charles tried to convey the sense that this was unrealistic. With the husband in the four-bedroom house and the wife in local authority accommodation, it seemed difficult to argue that she should not have at least a share in the equity. It might be difficult for the client to hang on to the house. The matter would now rest with the solicitor, who took the view that the husband's earning capacity should be protected and any property capable of increasing in value should be retained because 'even if she got the lion's share, it won't re-house her. And with her share, she won't be able to buy and maintain a mortgage, and the money (a lump sum) won't help her as she is on benefits'.

This was a sad case where too much money had been spent on legal advice. But it seemed unlikely that the couple could have benefited from mediation. The lack of trust was acute. The contribution of the barrister was to check the husband's financial position and convince the wife's legal team that there was no 'pot of gold'. Then he could put forward certain ideas (such as that the sale might be postponed until the wife could guarantee she could re-house herself and earn some income) so that negotiation could begin in the knowledge of what a judge was likely to do if agreement was not reached.

VI.   Graham: A Final Hearing with little on the table

The second 'no money' case also took place outside London. The researcher observed Graham, a young local barrister who had been given the papers the evening before. He was acting for the wife in a final hearing in the County Court. Until 5 pm the previous day he had been expecting to appear in care proceedings many miles away. He described it as 'the rough end of the family bar'. He had worked late and early, and when he met the researcher at court at 9 am he gave a summary of the case. It involved a couple with low incomes and extraordinary levels of personal debt (over £50,000 each), who were divorcing after 10 years of marriage. There were no children. The wife was earning under £3,000 per annum as a part-time beautician. She was still in the matrimonial home but unable to meet the mortgage repayments. Her original flat had been repossessed and was on the market. The husband, who was living with his new partner and baby in the new partner's accommodation, was hoping to earn £25,000 in a small business he had set up since being made redundant from his previous job. The issue was what to do about the home and the flat, and how to divide whatever small sums of money were available. The wife wanted to buy out the husband's share in the home so she could stay in it, and finance herself from sale of the flat and with help from friends and family. The husband wanted the home sold so he could get his share in the capital value. The finances were a tangle of mortgages, re-mortgages, undocumented debts to family members and agreements with credit card companies.

The client arrived with the young solicitor (who was not well prepared) at 9.30 for the 10.30 hearing. She was in an anxious state. Graham had to establish a relationship at his first meeting with her, attempt to make sense of the documents, try to clarify detail, fill gaps, and to understand what she wanted. He needed to make clear how large the gap might be between what she wanted and what a judge might order.

The case was legally aided on both sides, and the barrister remarked that there is no recognition in legal aid remuneration of late instructions for counsel, unlike the position for solicitors, who are compensated for emergency work on the grounds that they may have had to turn away other work. In this case the solicitor had presented a Form E financial statement which was a year old, and included a lot of historical data but nothing on the current position. The difficulties which this caused during the hearing provide compelling evidence of the disadvantages of 'juniorisation' in solicitors' practices.

The conversation with the client will not be presented in detail, but the following gives a flavour:

> Graham: 'The sale of the flat will attract Capital Gains Tax. What did you pay for it?' The client: '£330,000 plus £5,000 for work on it'. Graham: '£62,000 gain, £31,000 each'. Taking out a calculator: 'If we do rough figures, you're earning a small amount ... a 25 per cent tax payer. £5,000 tax . . . your allowance may cover it ... no order the court makes will affect that. Your current assets are? Current account?' The client: 'Nothing: £30 balance'. Graham asks about her liabilities. 'I see [X] sued you ... did he withdraw?' The client replies that this was her accountant: 'It's ok ... no liability for me'.

The usher then knocked on the interview room door and asked if there were any documents for the judge. Graham replied that he would prepare a summary as soon as he has been through the figures with the client. He then ran through the history of the flat and house, the mortgages and re-mortgages, and what the money released had been used for. The client wanted to stay in the house. The husband had apparently thought that she would get her original flat and that he would take the house, but this was complicated by the fact that she brought in the flat but he took over the mortgage, though there was rental income. Graham then said:

> The judge will be looking to reduce your debt. You must be paying a huge amount. The judge would say: 'Sell the house and divide the proceeds'. But you say that friends and family are willing to lend you enough to buy him out of the house. The starting point is to see what there is. He alleges you overspend. You say it was as a family.

'His spending was more than mine', replied the client. Graham asked the solicitor whether it was ever suggested that there should be narrative statements at the directions hearing. She said: 'No'. The client asked what that meant and Graham explained that this is the kind of case where the account needs to be fleshed out with the details of the story, but that 'we don't want to do that. Just say the indebtedness is joint and that you brought the flat to the marriage'. There followed discussion about expensive cars, and what happened to the husband's lump sum on retirement. He claimed to have spent it partly on credit card repayment, repayment to a relative, and on buying tools for his business and things for the new baby.

At 10.30 the usher asked if they were ready. The other barrister arrived. Both counsel said they were not ready, but would speak to the judge. They went in. The judge was firm and brusque, saying that with £120,000 in assets, and £100,000 liabilities, this was an argument about nothing. He was not prepared to let things go another day. He was not happy that there was no list of liabilities. Graham put forward his position, saying that the wife could borrow from family and friends. Sale of the home might be avoided. He apologised for having taken over the case at the last minute. The judge asked why this happened, as it was long standing case. 'That's life at the family bar'. But he gave a further 15 minutes.

> Graham and the barrister for the other side (from same chambers) confer. Running quickly through the figures, the other side say: 'I will ask for £8,000 to her. In exchange we get the home, and she gets the proceeds of sale of the flat. The way we get to that is … he brought in £11,000 deposit on the home, £13,000 endowment worth £45,000, mortgage £32,000: so the difference is £15,000. He says the properties are worth £134,000. I get the first £16,000 and we divide the rest. We say she caused the expenditure over the years'. Graham says: 'We have no narrative affidavits'. The barrister for the other side says: 'I have no bloody idea what went on'. Graham says: 'We're not pursuing conduct, but if there is a conduct argument on her I'm going to have to make a fuss because there were no narrative affidavits. I'll go to my client with your proposals and hope the judge will be reasonable and give us time'. The other barrister says: 'We're going into the dark!'

Graham returned to the client and asked for further details, but by this stage she was too upset to answer. The usher called them into court. Both barristers asked for another 15 minutes but the judge refused. The wife could not be found, as she had disappeared to the ladies' room. The proceedings recommenced at 11 am. The barrister for the husband opened. The judge intervened, saying that he needed to consider the husband's future earning capacity on which he had no information. He asked why there was no documentation about the lump sum redundancy payment. Counsel for the husband replied that there was documentation but that it was not disclosed. The judge said that in a case where there is no money and £24,000 had disappeared overnight, it was not helpful. He pointed out that the information in his bundle was 12 months old and asked where to find updated information. The barrister for the other side gave page references. The judge was surprised to see no disclosure for 12 months. A long silence followed.

In glacial tones, the judge continued, pointing out that the court was severely handicapped by lack of information, despite the parties having paid many thousands of pounds getting there. The hearing continued. Counsel for the husband set out her client's position. This was a short marriage. There were no children. Putting the debts on one side, the husband had contributed £11,000 to the home, £13,000 endowments cashed in, £7,000 on post-separation expenditure for the wife: that is £31,000. The wife had contributed a flat worth £45,000 in 1997, with a mortgage of £37,000, so bringing in £15,000. The husband had brought in £16,000 more, so their proposals in principle were that, taking the properties to be worth £134,000, the husband should take the first £16,000, and divide the remainder 50/50, save that the wife should allow the flat to be repossessed with reduction in value. The judge checked that there was no claim with respect to pensions and asked what was the basis for this contribution argument. Counsel responded that this was a short marriage with no children. Graham was asked for his view. He suggested that contributions were more or less equal. He did a calculation based on a current valuation of the flat by the bank at £98,000, which represented an annual increase in value of £4,000, and therefore her contribution on a crude basis was close to the husband's £31,000. The wife would like an order where assets were valued equally and she was given the opportunity to buy the husband out of the home.

The proceedings then went on to hear oral evidence from both parties, the judge intervening actively, requesting documentation on a number of issues, and indicating his lack of satisfaction with the evidence provided by both. As the judge pressed the husband on his spending, Graham interposed that he did not accuse the husband of concealing funds and accepted that the overspending was joint. The husband then tried to establish that the overspending was the wife's responsibility. Graham kept asking whether 'you both benefited', to which husband replied several times 'yes but not equally'. Graham said that the wife did not accept this, and asked whether affidavits might be needed. When the wife gave evidence, she was pressed by the other side and by the judge on the feasibility of her proposal that she should keep the house with the financial help from friends and family, and on her earning capacity. This followed her very confused responses on the details of past mortgage problems, and she was unable to provide any documentation in confirmation of these offers of help on how repayment would be made. The judge indicated that the case might need another few days, saying that for a contributions-based approach 'we'll need documents'. The court rose at 1 pm, to reconvene at 2.15. The judge told the wife, who was still giving evidence, not to talk to anyone.

In the interview room, Graham explained the husband's proposal in outline, and said that he did not expect her to agree. He did not give her the precise figures, as the judge had asked him not to do so while she was giving her evidence She confirmed she wanted a chance to stay in the house. Graham explained that the weakness in her position was factoring in the proportion of the redundancy money. Graham sent her out, so that he could consult with the other side. Counsel for the husband came in with more detail. They agreed that the judge would not want another day on this. 'No one does. It's legally aided. But it will be hard getting the figures right'. They both recalled that the judge was recently at the family bar doing finance.

> They go back into court. The judge grants five minutes for Graham to present the figures to the wife, which he had been asked not to do over the break. In the interview room, Graham suggests: 'We don't accept that the lump sum is spent. We suggest he keeps his liabilities, and gets the first £33,000 from the flat; the rest to you, maybe £13,000. You get the house and remove him from the mortgage. No maintenance or share of pension. You will have to pay your debts and find the mortgage. I can't see how we can settle. You can see the way the judge is working. He will impose a figure on you. But if the judge wants it neat this is neat'. The client says: 'Whatever', as long as she keeps the house. Graham says he thinks the judge does not believe that friends and family would bail her out.
>
> Everyone is called back into court at 3 pm. Graham summarises his position. He suggests that both were complicit in the overspending. He understands the judge's reservations about the soft finance, but would welcome a chance to buy out, limited to, say, three months. The judge responds that the mortgage would be £100,000, which she could not pay even if working full time. There is no way she can retain the house. This was not a short marriage, which would be one under five years. The court rises and the judge says he will return in 30 minutes.

Judgment was given at 4.15. The judge recited the detail of the assets and debts, income and earning capacity, and noted that the husband's partner was unlikely to return to work because of the children. The earning capacities of husband and wife were found to be broadly similar (around £25,000). The contributions were irrelevant, as this was not a short marriage. Both were found to have told the court bad things, and time had been wasted. The judge said that neither witness had been helpful or reliable in one of the worst prepared cases he had ever seen. There is no place for assessing contributions in other than a short marriage. He did not accept that the husband was ignorant of finances during the marriage. He did not accept that the wife's earning capacity was £3,000. He looked at the equity of £130,000, and, taking account of the pension lump sum, if the assets were to be divided equally, there would be £72,000 each, but the husband had the £15,000 pension lump sum, so this would not be just. Therefore 60 per cent of the house was to go to the wife and 40 per cent to the husband. The flat would be divided equally. There should be a clean break. Graham returned to the interview room at 4.30 to explain to the wife that she was looking to a sale of the house but that she would be free of debt. He said that she should not take the judge's comments to heart. He commented to the researcher that the judgment lay squarely between both positions, and that these were some of the harshest words he had ever heard in court. 'But the outcome is OK'.

This was a financially dysfunctional couple who had taken up entrenched positions and had been fighting all the way to a final hearing. Graham had to master a complex story rapidly, despite poor documentation and under heavy fire from an angry judge, with a distressed client seeking the impossible. The barrister seemed to accept the wife's instructions that he should seek to prevent sale of the house without much resistance, despite telling her that she was unlikely to succeed. The problems were exacerbated by having a junior solicitor handling a complex legal aid case with a difficult client. As in all the money cases observed, the barrister was acting as an auditor, checking and re-checking the financial information. But in this case it did not lead to further negotiation, partly due to lack of time, and partly due to the barrister's inability to talk the client around to a more favourable position. But that is very difficult at a contested final hearing.

VII.   Alice's 'Mediation'

We conclude with a 'medium' money case. The researcher observed Alice, an experienced woman barrister, out of London, who specialised in family law, but was not restricted to finance. She was representing the wife at an FDR. The husband was not represented. The wife was very distressed. Her husband had left her with two teenage children after a long marriage. She had a low-paid, part-time job. He had re-partnered and had a new baby. She kept returning to the fact that she had done nothing wrong. How was she to take care of the children? Where would she live? Alice met her in court, and had continually to soothe and reassure her while trying hard to clarify what exactly she was asking for. As the husband was unrepresented, she also had to advise him on procedure and the limits of what would be acceptable to a court if the matter did not settle, at the same time making it clear that she was not acting for him. The husband was angry with the barrister, who patiently started from considering what the children would need. She said: 'There is no magic wand to be waved here. There are limits and reasonableness unless you want a trial' At the word 'trial' the husband quietened down and agreed to make a list, and tell her the parameters for an arrange-ment. He wanted to bring his new partner into court. This caused great anxiety to the wife and was refused.

The client kept on asking for very little, and Alice had to explain that it was possible to bargain down but not up, so advised that perhaps she needed to set the original figure higher. Alice expected the outcome to be 25 per cent equity of the house to the husband, the remainder and maintenance of £1,200 a month to the wife. 'That will leave some for him and the judge will agree. We can't take all the money. You just can't'. The husband was objecting to the £1,200, and accused the wife of being a spendthrift. The barrister calmly persuaded the wife that the judge was likely to order 25 per cent capital (which husband had accepted) and the £1,200 maintenance.

This was what was agreed at the FDR. The role of the barrister in this case was, as always, first to get the figures straight. Then, because the husband was unrepresented, she essentially played the role of a media-tor, skilled in the details of divorce finances. She had the advantage of having a clear idea of what the judge would accept, and carefully drew both sides closer and closer to this position while soothing and keeping them focused on the essential financial issues.

5

Children Cases: Contact

I. Introduction

WHEN WE ANALYSED the information collected while observing the work of the family law barristers, we expected to distinguish between divorce-related and child protection work. That would reflect the traditional division between private and public law cases. Although financial and child issues are treated separately in divorce, the needs of the children do in fact play a key role in property division, particularly as more fathers now seek accommodation which is suitable to allow children to stay overnight and for longer periods. Furthermore, although child maintenance is regarded by the justice system as separate from contact and residence issues, recent research commissioned by One Parent Families[1] shows that some parents view them as being interrelated. But because any child maintenance issues included in a consent order would be dealt with within ancillary relief for married parents, and other cases are dealt with outside the court by the Child Support scheme, private law children cases are mostly about contact and residence. We therefore decided to examine this aspect of family law advocacy separately from that concerning financial arrangements.

Having made this decision, it seemed logical to separate the private and public law children cases. The private law cases include issues between parents in making arrangements for continuing parenting after separation. Public law cases are about the state's intervention to protect children at risk of abuse or neglect, and to make plans for their care. But even this distinction is a thin one. Contact cases do not arise only between a child's parents. They may arise between the parents and other

---

[1] OPF Report by J Hunt and V Peacey, *Problematic contact after separation and divorce? A national survey of parents* (July 2008).

relatives, or with a foster parent. Disputes between parents are some-times characterised as being about adults having foolish arguments about the time they spend with their children, and questions might be raised about the desirability of limiting the amount of public funding to be made available for this kind of dispute. There is a policy commit-ment to offering in-court conciliation to encourage mediation between these parents.[2] Yet Buchanan, Bretherton, and Hunt have revealed the seriousness of the contact disputes which come to court. They observed that the levels of stress among children involved in contact disputes equalled those of children involved in care proceedings.[3] Similarly, in her study of in-court conciliation, Trinder found that in many cases fear of the other parent's poor parenting accounted for maternal reluctance to agree contact, particularly overnight unsupervised contact.[4] We came across the same types of issue in the cases we describe below. The seriousness of these cases should not be underestimated.

II. Jane and the Unrepresented Foster Parent

Although this case was not a dispute between the child's parents, it had many of the features of such a dispute. The barrister, Jane, who was based outside London, was a specialist in children cases with a strong interest in mediation. Her client was a single mother in case before a Family Proceedings Court outside the capital. The client had given her nine-year-old son to friends three years ago with a view to adoption. The child was currently being cared for under a residence order. The mother and foster parents had become estranged, and the child had recently asked to live with his mother. The mother was willing to take him back, and had applied for a residence order, but after interviews with officers from the Children and Family Courts Advisory and Support Service (CAFCASS) and expert assessments, the child had changed his mind. The matter was now about contact between the mother and the child.

The papers had arrived at 4 pm the previous day. Jane had worked on them until 11 pm, and one file remained unread. The hearing was set

---

[2]   L Trinder and J Kellett, *The longer term consequences of in-court conciliation* (Ministry of Justice, 2007)

[3]   A Buchanan, J Hunt, H Bretherton, and V Bream, *Families in Conflict, Perspectives of Children and Parents on the Family Court Welfare Service* (Bristol, Policy Press, 2001).

[4]   See above n 2.

for 10 am. There were issues about the mother's wish to involve the child in sporting activities, while the foster parents wished to encourage his musical abilities and the two activities clashed at weekends. The matter in dispute was the timetabling of contact during weekends. The area of disagreement did not seem great. Jane had in mind a family assistance order (FAO)[5] to help matters go smoothly, and when the researcher met her at the court at 9.30, she was checking to see whether such an order could be made without the presence of Social Services.

The client arrived, an interview room was found, and Jane showed her the summary she had prepared for the judge. The mother queried one line, which Jane crossed out and agreed to explain why to the judge. The solicitor for the guardian *ad litem* was present and brought in a draft schedule for contact prepared by the foster parents. The foster father was there, but without legal representation. The foster parents had raised objections to the child being taken to parties with adults by his mother. Jane presented this information to the mother, and sought to diffuse the dispute by joking about family parties. The mother described how the foster mother had packed a smart shirt, indicating her consent to the outing. Jane reassured her, saying that the foster parents/parent relationship is often a difficult one, that the foster parents had not been supported in this role and that their anger was not unusual. The mother was also upset by the description of her in the expert report. Jane persuaded the mother to consider an FAO, and asked about mediation. The client agreed to the FAO, but said that the foster parents would refuse mediation. Jane then went to speak to the foster father. He appeared tight- lipped and angry. Jane stressed that she was looking for something which would work better in the future, not just a deal for the day. Meanwhile the guardian's solicitor said the guardian would only agree to be named in the FAO if it was focused on better communication through round table meetings.

The usher came to say that the judge was asking where they were. Jane suggested going in and telling him where they had got to. The case was listed for one and a half days, but she thought: 'We can get it sorted'. She told the judge:

---

[5] Under a Family Assistance Order a CAFCASS officer or local authority can be required to be available 'to advise, assist and (where appropriate) befriend anyone named in the order': Children Act 1989 s 16(1). They may only be made in exceptional circumstances, and require the consent of everyone named in the order (eg the local authority) other than the child. They are limited to six months.

We have reached a large measure of agreement. The residence application by the mother has been withdrawn because she is conscious of how the child is suffering as a result of what is being said. There is agreement for six visits, three of which are to be staying weekends, a year—schedule to be agreed— and a proposal for an FAO. There are details capable of resolution and we may not need resolution by the court.

She asked for more time. The judge checked with the foster father, and agreed, saying that this was a boy approaching a sensitive age who needed an arrangement which was both structured and flexible as his needs changed. The guardian's solicitor argued that there was need for an order as the parties were unable to work together. He was ambivalent about the FAO, and said that the schedule was the sticking point.

The judge described the child as walking a tightrope, trying to meet everybody's needs. He emphasised that the court should pay careful attention to what the child said, and should be thinking about asking the mother to structure the weekend with activities he liked so he could look forward to it, and also give the child a get out if he didn't feel like it. An FAO for six months would help him to be confident in saying what he wanted. He finished by saying: 'If possible, give him (the foster father) a piece of paper to sign, hopefully by 1 pm', and he left the parties to get on with it.

At 10.45 Jane arranges meetings with the client in the child care room, the guardian and her solicitor in the court, and the foster father in the lobby. She goes through the foster father's draft schedule with the mother. There are conflicts between football and concerts, and restrictions on taking the child to the pub after matches. At 11.05 the solicitor and guardian want to discuss the FAO. The client says, sadly: 'I feel I'm the only person giving way so (the child) is not pulled to pieces'. The guardian asks whether they want to agree a past history. The client says: 'No, the past is the past'. They discuss phone contact, and the solicitor for the guardian accuses the client, saying: 'When I ask you about the future you talk about the past'. Jane is quick to defend her client saying: 'No, she's giving context'. The FAO is drafted jointly. The guardian agrees it should be child-centred and with achievable objectives. Jane agrees the draft, but then goes on to the schedule, wanting the guardian to understand why she is seeking changes, saying it was 'not to be awkward, but because of mum's work'. (The mother is a nurse). It is now time to show the schedule to the foster father. The guardian says they should all meet together. But Jane says: 'He's representing himself, so ...'. She prefers to keep the appropriate boundaries, without upsetting the guardian. Jane goes to see the foster father at 12.30. She tells him she has been through his draft schedule with mum and has some suggestions. He objects to each date, drags up the past when messages were lost, says he is not sure of half-term dates, and keeps referring to rehearsals and concerts, but cannot find the dates and does not have the a phone number to inquire. Jane offers to get it, but he mumbles about answer-phones, and talks about the child having had an unhappy Christmas with his mother. Jane says she is not asking for contact over Christmas. He objects to phone calls in the evening because the child has to go to bed at 7 30. He says: 'If (the child) doesn't want to do any of these and says he's not going he'll have to talk to his mum on the phone'. Jane replies: 'It's going to cut both ways. He may want more time. My client has withdrawn her residence application. This is going to be the minimum'. Jane is unfailingly calm and pleasant. Finally the foster father says: 'Ok'.

Jane returns to the mother and goes through the dates. The client is anxious about having enough notice of weekend visits to arrange her work schedules. Jane tells her to be careful, as it would be difficult to agree dates and then ask to change. 'We can show some room to manoeuvre now, flexibility will creep in'. The mother then agrees the dates. Jane goes back to the foster father and the guardian's solicitor, and the schedule is agreed. The usher asks about progress. The judge gives an extra five minutes. Jane says: 'I'll start writing at lightning speed, but will need to run the words past my client'. The foster father is still grumbling: 'He's been to parties up till 2 or 3 in the morning'. Jane says: 'I'm going to have to go and draft somewhere else. I'll do it faster'. It is now 12.45. Jane comes back with the draft at 1.05 and checks one last point with the guardian. The foster father wants one more safe-guard: if the child stays with someone else they need to know. The mother says: 'What if I have flu?' All this is dealt with by agreeing a phone call before visits. Everyone goes into court and the judge says: 'Thank you, you've done all the work. I'm sure this is the best arrangement to meet (the child's) needs. My last word is "be flexible". I make the orders'. Outside Jane has a last word with her client and says that it may always be frosty, but she should think ahead: 'You will need to communicate'.

As in the case reported at 4.VII, Jane was the only barrister present. Like Alice in that case, Jane needed to master the detail, fix in her mind the requirement to put the welfare of the child first, keep her client calm, and assuage the concerns of the unrepresented foster father. She was an unusually gifted and sensitive negotiator, almost a counsellor. The matter was much helped by the flexibility of the judge, who in turn was helped by the speed of settlement. They not only agreed a schedule for future arrangements, but the long-term support of the FAO. This was all achieved in a morning. It is hard to see how such a good outcome could have been achieved in any other way.

III. David and the Three-year Old with a Short Fuse

David was a senior junior of 15 years call, based outside London, specialising in children cases. In this case he was acting for the mother, who was unhappy about the father's request for unsupervised and staying contact with a child of three who had a speech impediment. She did not object to the child seeing his father, and indeed had older children by a previous partner who regularly spent time with this father. But the child's speech difficulty made it hard for him to express himself, and when frustrated he became difficult. He was improving, but she was afraid that the father would not be able to handle the situation if the child had a tantrum, and would be hard on him. At present contact was regular, but took place in a children's centre with a relative present in the background. The father now wanted to take the boy home, and had agreed to attend parenting classes to improve his ability to handle any problems.

David arrived at the court (outside London) at 9.45 am, met the client and her sister, and found a room. He had seen the client at a previous hearing, but now made a great effort to win her confidence, telling her about his own children, sitting on the floor, and saying that he was writing a book about this kind of work. The client was nervous and asked what was going to happen. David answered: 'We all have points to make. Family law is not confrontational. Everyone is pro contact'. The mother grumbled that the father was only going to the parenting classes because of the court case. Playing down the client's expression of distrust of the other party, David said: 'Ok, but we'll assume it's genuine, and then say that if he needs the classes then he's not yet ready for it (unsupervised contact)'. He suggested:

> We need to take small steps. It will come back to court in a few months. We need to know how long the classes are for, and if they are appropriate for (the child's) needs. The barrister representing dad is a colleague. If he's reasonable … but she's stuck with her instructions if he wants to fight … but I want to go away with a plan.

> David shows his outline to the client and her sister, both of whom say it's really good. 'There's nothing else you can say or do … it's for (the child's)

welfare'. David raises the question of the father's mother. The client says she is 'manipulating and controlling … she's behind all the pushing'. David asks how she would be as a carer for a short time. The client says she would just take over. David asks: 'Would it be better for (the child) if he has a tantrum if granny's there? Leaving aside your personal feelings for her?' The client says that, after having contact for two years (the child) doesn't call his father 'dad'. 'He calls everyone dad'. David warns that this argument could backfire, 'if we start from the point that a child should have a meaningful relationship with his father'. The mother's sister says that at contact the boy goes straight up to his dad. David tries to explain the father's point of view, saying: 'Maybe he feels a bit disempowered', while also supporting his client and her sister: 'The two of you do a fantastic job'. He gently leads the mother to look forward, saying that there will eventually be a move away from supervised contact, either as the father gets more capable or (the child) gets older.

When the solicitor arrived at 10 am, David brought her up to date. He explained his negotiating strategy.

We had a chat with you (the client) and my colleague will have had a chat with him (the father). In a while I'll go and have a chat with her (the opposing barrister) and we'll see if we can agree. Can you remind yourself of your statements? But if it does come to evidence, I won't go over the case (ie the past).

The client took the point, and said: 'When I saw his statement it was all about the past … a good old slanging match'. David congratulated her: 'Yours is excellent … child-centred', and went to fetch coffees. Then David saw the father's counsel and solicitor. They said they would not seek a change in contact arrangements today. The parenting course would start soon and last seven weeks. If it went well, they would seek to move to unsupervised contact. It would begin in the Children's Centre, then they would go to the park alone, then back while the sister stayed in the Centre. David said he would be seeking a reassurance that the father completed the course and had been fully engaged with it. He returned, and the client and her sister are happy with this. He obtained their agreement to send the child's medical reports to the course educational psychiatrist. The CAFCASS officer looked in for an update and went off to find the father.

The client's anxieties reappear. 'What if it doesn't work'? Her sister adds: 'It's been a long haul. We just want to be safe'. David: 'Then we come back to court … but you don't want to *keep* coming back to court. Most single mums look forward to a breather'. David then starts to plan a detailed timetable. 'Dad's course finishes on 3 August, so it's every first and third Saturday, and so our first slightly unsupervised contact would be… half an hour in the middle of the visit? 45 minutes? Then an hour, hour and a half?' The client's sister asks if someone will write it down for her so that she will get it right. David, while urging caution and patience, says that there may be teething problems. The sister becomes more positive and says it should be fine. '(The child) can come back and have tea with the other children. Teething problems can be dealt with as they come'. But the mother is getting nervous. It is 10.30. David says: 'This is how I propose to draft it. Stage one—as we come up to that first contact—30 minutes, then 45, then an hour, an hour and a half, then three hours and then such contact as you can agree'. The mother agrees. David concludes: 'We could say more, but we don't want to push'. (As so often, the form of speech used by counsel refers to 'we', not 'I').

The client and her sister left the interview room so that David could talk with the father's legal advisers. He made the proposals described above, and added:

> While on the course we stick with the course . . . on condition dad is engaged and attends as evidenced by a written report, and the psychologist's report is fine, and the build up … I can't push her beyond that, but she is delighted he is going on the course, they would like it to happen … she describes her aim as trying to build that (contact) up so that it doesn't fall down.

Notice how the barrister refers to the goals he suggested to his client as originating from the client. Counsel for the father said they would have to go back and check what was needed, as he might want three hours. They agreed a date for the report. David checked that the course was suitable for the parent of a child of this age, and it appeared that it was the only course that could be found. The father's lawyers left. David said to the solicitor: 'I'll agree something platitudinous for stage three, like unsupervised contact in excess of two hours if stage two is ok and by agreement, to give father a framework too, but preserve our safety net'. The father's barrister returned, saying that the father was happy with the progression, and asked if it was time to speak to CAFCASS. David said he needed to tell his client. Then the father's counsel slipped in that he would like to bring another family member at, say, the two-hour stage … grandma!

> David replies that this should happen while the sister is still involved. The other barrister says, more firmly, that they would expect to involve another family member at the two-hour stage. David says he will speak to his client and they should see CAFCASS together. The mother and sister come back from the coffee shop, and David explains the timetable,

going up to two hours, but says they are keen to get to three hours. The mother asks: 'Can we see how it goes?' David says that he has floated stage three, and hopes it will go well, but that precise arrangements could be taken to court for review if needed. The client would prefer a report from CAFCASS, and all contact near her home. Then David says: 'Another thing ... we anticipated this', but before he can say more the sister interjected: 'His mother!' David says that the father is asking to bring another family member with him, and moves to head off a possible obstacle to agreement being created by his client: 'I know ... even if you don't like her. But if (the child) throws a wobbly . . .'. The mother says: 'Can we see how it goes and introduce his mother after the review?' David skillfully points out the difficulty with that: 'Once we move away from three hours . . . if we see grandma as a safeguard, we want her in place sooner. I think if you introduce somebody new ... there is nothing unusual about this, you want to do it when there is reassurance, while your sister is there—that is my gut instinct' .The client quickly picks up this suggestion, saying: 'Then my sister can assess and tell me'. David follows up: 'Your sister can say: "Here's daddy's mummy"'. At this point the client gives in, saying: 'It seems to me it's going to happen. So long as everything is in place I'll go along with it'. David: 'It's a bit of a leap of faith, contact ... but if things go wrong we can bring it back (to court). If we take a pessimistic view it will never happen'.

It was 11.30. The usher came to ask them to be in court at 12 noon. David told him the time would be productive and there would probably be agreement. David reminded the client that the father had agreed to all their requests, and couldn't have been more compliant. She replied: 'I'm happy with that'. Her sister then became anxious, wondering: 'What if he doesn't get on with the course?' David reassured them both: 'We've asked for a letter to go to court. It's a serious thing. We want updates'. On her way in to court, the client said to David: 'Now I've spoken to you ... you've done it all these years ... your experience ... I'm quite at ease now. It's a relief'. David assured her that they would tie up all the loose ends in a rock-solid agreement: 'We'll go before the judge and he'll tell us all how wonderful we are'.

After a short discussion between both sides and CAFCASS, who needed some persuasion, and a visit to the listing office to set a date for return and review, and a trip to chambers over the road to type up the order, this is exactly what happened. The barrister's skills had gradually created in the client a feeling of trust and confidence, overcome her hostility and promoted an understanding of the parameters of what was possible and desirable for the child. There was a carefully-staged, clear timetable, with safeguards. The client left feeling that she had achieved the best outcome for her child. It was a good morning's work.

IV Jonathan and the Concerned Mother

The two cases considered above involved negotiation. The third case, however, is different in structure and character because it involved a full hearing on a matter of fact. Jonathan was a junior barrister called to the bar five years ago, who worked from London. The case was heard outside London. He was representing a mother who was convinced that her former husband had touched one of the children inappropriately and wanted the court to make a finding of fact that this had occurred. The father, as part of his claim for contact, sought a finding that this had not taken place. This was therefore an accusation of criminal behaviour, which the mother needed to support with evidence. Her problem, however, was that the evidence was very thin. A two-day hearing had been listed. The character of the process was closer to criminal proceedings than a family law matter.

In describing the case to the researcher, Jonathan described his client as having a long and happy marriage. There were two boys, aged four and six at the time of the incident. The mother believed that, on going up to the bedroom one evening to call her husband for his meal, she saw him on the bed with one of the boys touching him in an inappropriate way. She effectively ended the marriage immediately, but continued to allow access by the father to the children in her presence at weekends. He had consistently denied the allegations. The boys had 'disclosed' to the mother the day after her concerns arose, and later to their maternal grandmother, but had not done so to the specialist Woman Police Constable (WPC). So there was no effective corroboration, or physical evidence, to support mother's claims. She agreed that her husband had always been a loving father, and she did not want to stop him seeing the children altogether, but was not willing for him to see them on his own.

Jonathan, who had seen the client once previously, met her at court at 9.30. She looked nervous but smart in a black suit almost like a lawyer's. The solicitor arrived at 10 am. Jonathan chatted about the cold weather, needing his old sweater, etc, putting her at her ease. He began to go through the witness statement, anticipating potential cross-examination: 'Can we run over the facts? How would you describe your relationship with your husband?' She replied: 'I thought we were happy'. Jonathan circled around before raising the problems in the marriage: 'You went to Relate some years ago?' This not only informs Jonathan, but also enables the client to rehearse her answers, in preparation for giving evidence. She replied: 'That was a long time ago. He was drinking ... stressed ... family illness'. Jonathan then turned to specific detail of the day in question. 'When you got up to the room, was the door open?' 'Ajar ... stuff on the back, it doesn't shut'. Jonathan asked: 'Had you seen him lying on the bed on previous occasions?' 'Not really ... it's bunks ... if you sit on it you bang your head'. Jonathan: 'Was he on the bed or sitting on the floor?' 'Not sure'. Jonathan: 'Could you see his hands?' 'Can't remember. It was the atmosphere. Something wasn't right'. Jonathan: 'When you spoke to L (son), you asked if daddy had tickled his back or his tummy. Did you mention willy or bum?' 'No. I asked him to show me and he pointed ... he couldn't say it'.

Jonathan then asked detailed questions about whether the boys ever played games of a sexual nature, about what the boys had said to her and to their grandmother, and what they said to the WPC. The client became upset and said: 'I was in shock ... clutching at straws ... I don't see why I should make it up'. Further questions and answers followed about the boys' behaviour and progress at school, the brief return of the father to the former matrimonial home, and the agreement that there would be no touching or bathing. Jonathan was very thorough, going through every aspect of the arguments he might want to make, and also any questions which he expected might come from the other side.

The usher came to get the names of witnesses. Jonathan asked for a further 15 minutes. He then went through the grandmother's evidence with her. She asked what would happen if the decision was for the father, and what would happen if it happened again? Jonathan explained that if there was an allegation at any time it would be investigated. He then returned to the client and said:

> Let's have a little chat about what will happen today, what our thoughts are. We'll go into court, I'll open the case. It's about findings. I'm not applying, but I have to prove ... provide evidence. The court has to be satisfied. These are serious allegations so there has to be very strong evidence. As I've said to you before, the evidence here is very weak, only disclosure by the children, no other evidence, as so often. It makes these cases very difficult. They will say that because there have been lots of questions to the children that they've got muddled. If you repeat things they say it back. We won't be able to prove any of this. I'd put my pension on it, if I had one. So its up to you ... what do we do? Either we can go through with the hearing, which will be upsetting for

all. More information might come out in the witness box. But if I'm right, we could withdraw and the judge could go on to order some contact, probably unsupervised, but going slowly. Another way of looking at it is to go ahead. I think we won't be successful. A hearing will make the situation worse and make contact more difficult. The advantage of going ahead is psychological for you. You'll feel you have done everything you can. There are advantages and disadvantages on both sides. It's for you to make the decision. He will be looking for unsupervised contact. There is supervised contact now.

The mother asked: 'What about a CAFCASS report? They're happy if it carries on supervised'. Jonathan agreed that that was important, but warned that there would be delay, and that the judge would seek early contact. He said:

> CAFCASS is very important, it makes a report to the court and the court has to say why if it doesn't accept the recommendations. You could say: 'I won't go through with the hearing and accept limited contact until CAFCASS reports', or go ahead… it's up to you.

The client replied 'I know it's hard to prove. That's the only evidence there could be. It's lucky for my children I stopped it. I know it happened and I'll do whatever I can to make it safe for them'. She appeared quiet and sad. Then she added: 'I haven't poisoned the kids against him. That's why I go for two hours every Wednesday and five hours on Saturday'.

At 10.38 the usher said that the judge wanted everyone in, and that he would give more time but 'you have to ask for it'. All the parties went in. The judge ran through the list of witnesses and possible timings. Jonathan said that he expected to finish on the following day. He had to apologise, as his pagination was one digit out (he did it himself). The judge asked whether the mother had thought about contact being extended and unsupervised. Jonathan replied that there were matters to consider. The judge then asked if the boys wanted more contact. Jonathan replied that his understanding was that they wanted the same, and with their mother present. The judge granted 15 minutes. Outside the courtroom, the client said admiringly to Jonathan: 'I don't know how you do it … banging on'. Jonathan was pleased that the judge seemed on top of the case, though he had wanted more time to go through the father's statement. He reminded the mother to pop to the loo, and did the same. He told her that when they go in he will ask her to look at her statement, and asked whether there was anything in particular she would like him to ask the father. He added: 'Sometimes barristers think they have thought of everything … but …'.

It is time to go into court. Jonathan whispers to the researcher that the judge is high powered. He has looked him up on the internet. His trouble is that he doesn't 'have anything'. He speaks briefly to the other counsel about agreeing statements, in which case the witness need not be called, but there are some questions for one witness. Jonathan opens, thanking the judge for the extra time, and giving an outline of the case. He says he is seeking a general finding of inappropriate touching. The WPC is called. Jonathan explores why no video was made, the difference between the boys' accounts, her level of experience, and her view that the older boy's later disclosure was on the mother's instructions. She is a very professional witness, answering the question but saying as little as possible. She is not to be dissuaded from her view that there had been no need to take further action. Jonathan then calls the mother. He takes her through the history of the relationship, and the events on the evening in question. She says: 'I said: "What are you doing in the bed with your son?" I just felt uneasy. He jolted up'. She then went downstairs. She says the father knew she wasn't happy. She intended to ask the boys about it the next day, when dad was at work, to put her mind at rest. She describes how the older boy could see what the younger one was describing, pointing at his bum, in the mirror. The judge swiftly intervenes to check that this is in her statement and that, if not, the other barrister has been notified. The court is about to rise for lunch. The mother is asked not to discuss her evidence over the break. The judge is very concerned about how far Jonathan is going to depart from the witness statement. His response is: 'Not intentionally' but there are things he hasn't heard before and, given the court's inquisitorial role, it is better to have all the cards on the table. The judge requires him to indicate which paragraphs in the statement would be involved. Jonathan offers to provide new evidence to counsel for the father over lunch.

Returning to the interview room, Jonathan explained that what he was doing was 'slightly naughty', in trying to 'take the sting' out of the other side's position. If points are aired before opposing counsel raises them they are less powerful. This technique is used in criminal proceedings. In the café, both barristers talked together of their despair about their cases. Both expected no finding either way, and unsupervised contact soon. On the way back to court, Jonathan whispered that civil procedure regarding evidence is more flexible in family matters, but that he might have to resort to an old criminal trial trick if the judge restricts his questions, and say: 'Are you asking me to say that …?'

At 2.15 Jonathan resumes his examination of the mother, going through what she had said to the children, when she first heard about some of the worrying incidents from the police who interviewed the children. Counsel for the father then examines her. He asks how the bedtime routine with their father usually went, establishing whether bedroom doors were open or closed, lights on or off etc, trying to make a point out of the fact that she went downstairs after seeing what worried her and carried on as usual. Why was this? Why does she think the elder boy did not describe what happened in full to the WPC? The mother answers: 'What child would want to say these things to a stranger?' When pressed on whether he had said dad touched his bum or the line of his bum she says that she could not remember. The judge insists that she must answer. Counsel presses on about when she was upset, when the boys were upset, whether the elder boy tended to imagine things, and why did she take the father back into the house for short time if she thought he was an abuser? She replies that at least she could see what went on if he was in the house and it was only for a few days. The judge intervenes to ask counsel whether it was his case that the mother did not believe it happened? Counsel replies: 'I accept she believed it at the time'. The judge asks whether he accepts that what she says the boys said, they did say. Jonathan immediately has a long exchange with the other barrister. The mother looks furious. Jonathan then says that counsel wishes to clarify what the mother heard from the children. By this time the mother is getting tired, and counsel is suggesting that she is being obstructive.

Questioning ends at 3.40. The Family Support worker is then called, and describes her five sessions with the boys, and says that because of disclosure to her she visited the grandmother's house with a WPC. There are some discrepancies between her account of the day when the older boy spoke of the events to the support worker and the mum's recollection. Counsel establishes from the support worker that mum said to her that the boy had something to tell her. Mum denies this, just that she told him to speak freely to the support worker. The grandmother is then called, and describes what the boys had said to her, and how the older boy played with his penis, saying daddy did this. The court rises at 4 pm, to reconvene and hear from the father the next morning.

Jonathan arrived just in time, saying he had missed his earlier train by one minute. He broke the tension with more jokes about his old jumper. He tried to comfort his client:

> You are shattered. At least there will be some finality today. I'm going to tell you my questions for (the father) and perhaps you can assist me. He'll tell his side of the story, like you did yesterday, then final points from both of us. It will be short; all the evidence is there from yesterday. The judge will make his decisions. We want a finding of touching on the penis. They want the judge to say he definitely did not, so you've got 'yes, he did' or 'no, he didn't' or 'not

enough evidence to say he didn't'. I think there's not enough evidence to say 'yes, he did', or he may say it's more complicated and he wants more time to think about it and he'll write it and send it. A CAFCASS report will be considered as well after the findings. We say the boys want to see him but with you there. Now, the question may seem odd, but was he sent away at any time? Are there any convictions?

The client replied that when he was 14, the father was sent to a borstal. Jonathan went through more details about the incident. He then went to talk to the other counsel, giving notice of his questions, but saying he didn't have much to ask the father. Then he returned to the conference room and his client. He thanked his solicitor for the attendance note she had taken yesterday, which was very helpful and in lovely handwriting. He observed that it is impossible to take a note of what is going on while examining a witness. He explained to the mother: 'I'm just having a think about everything' and sat drafting questions in silence under the gaze of the client, the solicitor, and the researcher. The mother was praying. The other side knocked on the door with answers to the questions about borstal. There was no indication that their client had suffered any abuse himself. Jonathan said: 'OK, but you know the stats, if he had been in care …'. When the opposing barrister left, Jonathan said he would leave out that submission, because it would lose the sympathy of the judge. He sighed: 'No time to write as always', as the usher knocked at 10 30.

Everyone goes into court. The judge enters and plugs in his laptop. The father takes the witness stand. His counsel takes him through his statement. All allegations are vigorously denied. He stresses his complete abhorrence of child abuse. He tells a sad story of living in his car after leaving the home, only being able to see the boys under her eye; of wanting to save the marriage. Jonathan is reprimanded by the judge for passing notes to his client and distracting the witness. Jonathan protests that there is new material, and he needed to take instructions. A 15 minute break is taken. Jonathan says to the mother: 'I know it's emotional but you're not doing yourself any favours. The rosary is ok here but not in court. What was upsetting you?' 'It's just listening to him lying', she replies. Jonathan moves to counteract the growth of hostile feelings against the father: 'When people say something wrong in the witness box it's usually a mistake, not lying. That's a rule of thumb'. But his client refutes another detail about watching videos. Jonathan says that this is 'not a killer point'.

At 11.45 everyone goes back in to court. The father is sitting alone in the witness box. The two barristers are laughing together. The Judge and his laptop return. Jonathan takes the father through the history of the happy relationship, then presses about the number of times he said he had lain on the bed with the boys at bedtime. 'You have said "I'm on the bed 100 times", then "five times". Is it five or 100?' The father swears the five is a lie. He says he has lain on the bed 100 times. Jonathan presses: 'A mistake or a lie?' The father: 'I said it wrong'. Jonathan pursues the point: 'How many lies have you told? Can we assume a lot of things are not true?' 'No'. 'Did you get into the bed?' 'I can't answer. I can't remember'. 'Were you asleep?' The father agrees he might have nodded off. Jonathan says: 'Is that a convenient way to explain jerking up?' The other counsel challenges, but Jonathan has his note on this and the judge accepts the question. Jonathan then takes the father though a number of detailed questions, for example, about how he said the boys were honest (implying that they would not exaggerate) and then comes to the point about touching the penis. He tries to establish consistency between what the boys have said to their mother, the grandmother and the support worker, and asks the father to explain this. The father's answer is that it all comes from the mother. But Jonathan says that this doesn't explain why on that Monday morning, in a happy household, in a happy marriage, the mother makes something up. 'I think she got an idea into her head and fuelled it', the father conjectures. Jonathan then goes through a number of points about the boys touching themselves, having irregular bedtimes, taking their pants down (the judge required references). The father admitted exaggeration. Jonathan quickly points out that these exaggerations help his case. The father says wearily: 'You can say what you wish, but I never hurt my children. I wanted to save my marriage'.

The final submissions followed. Counsel for the father said that the burden of proof about touching the penis rested with the mother. There was no precision. It would be difficult for a court to make such a finding and he mentioned a House of Lords' case on standard of proof, where Lord Nicholls said that the more serious the allegation the more unlikely it was that the event occurred. She also referred to guidance in *Rayden*[6] on leading questions, arguing that in this case her client had been seriously led. She insisted that there was no evidence that the father was touching the boys, and that subsequent evidence had been contaminated by the mother's questioning. She said that the mother appeared to lie about her presence in the support worker's room when disclosure was made. She finished by saying:

---

[6] *Rayden on Divorce* is a leading practitioner's textbook.

Your Honour's options are to find it occurred, find it did not, or to make no findings. I suggest you find it did not happen because a court ought to reach finality. There will be further proceedings about contact, and these would be helped by a clear finding now. The court has full evidence, and can make a finding now that will help the boys in the future.

Jonathan responded to the point about finality robustly, saying that a finding would be just a step. If the court were to make a finding of no case, 'are you saying that this can prevent any future proceedings about the boys? What practical effect could a finding have on a CAFCASS report?' The judge adjourned until 2 pm.

At 2.20 the usher calls everyone in. Jonathan rises to make his final submission. 'The mother's only aim has been to protect her children. I won't raise points of law, the evidential base is a narrow one, and there is no physical evidence'. The judge: 'I did not expect any'. Jonathan goes on: 'There has been some criticism of mum concerning her questions to the children. I am happy to make a concession: maternal instincts override best legal practice. She passionately wanted to get to the bottom of what happened to the children. We accept credulity is diminished. But I caution the court against seeing that she had a predisposition to see sexual abuse. This was a happy family'. The judge reminds Jonathan that the WPC has said there was no disclosure. Jonathan responds that 'in a flurry of activity ...with a house full of strangers . . . confusion ...this is not surprising'. He reminds the court that 'what came across in grandma's evidence was the clarity ... the specific hand movement ... my submission is there is a consistent thread'. The judge is critical and Jonathan admits that this is not his best point. He goes on to say: 'A better point is—why on earth would a mother want to make these allegations? She did not go upstairs looking for abuse. And the father did exaggerate ... a lie'. Finally the judge says that this is not a straightforward matter, and he will try to prepare the judgment this afternoon or will send it. Jonathan repeats that a CAFCASS report would be appropriate. The court rises. In the conference room, the mother says: 'I'm overwhelmed. I've done my best'. Jonathan advises her to try and wind down and stick to the arrangements. 'Don't discuss it with him'. The mother says: 'We don't speak'.

The written judgment was sent later, and made no finding either way. What had Jonathan achieved? Through careful presentation and testing of evidence he had enabled his client to put forward her best case. He had made sure that she knew what was going on and why, and did not have unrealistic expectations of the outcome. He supported her with sensitivity throughout what was, for her, an emotional roller-coaster for two days. He dampened down her feelings of hostility toward the father brought on by his testimony, knowing full well that the couple would need to co-operate over future contact. He did not acquire a 'conviction' in the form of a finding of fact desired by his client, but he had helped a distressed mother to feel that she had done all she could do to protect her boys, as she saw it. And the matter was not closed. And she left with some confidence that 'he will never ever do it again'.

6

Child Protection Cases

I. Introduction

C ONCERN ABOUT THE way that care cases are handled by local authorities and the justice system is longstanding. This is partly because the individuals concerned experience multiple problems. For the parents, these may include substance and alcohol abuse, mental illness, other health issues, violent behaviour, child sexual abuse, debt, housing difficulties, illiteracy and special needs, lack of sustained supportive relationships, children born to women by different fathers, and poor relationships with those in a position to help in the local authority and health services. For the children, there may be issues about abuse, neglect, ill-health and behaviour. The work involved in trying to support these parents and safeguard these children is so complex that it is hardly surprising that success is more of an aspiration than a reality in most cases, and that there will continue to be debate about how best to deal with them. Dame Margaret Booth's report in 1996[1] voiced concerns about the time taken to reach decisions. The Lord Chancellor's Department Scoping Study of 2002[2] was followed by the development of the Protocol for Judicial Case Management in Public Law Children Act Cases. This set out to improve judicial case management and speed up the process. But any attempt at speed risks cutting corners and either failing to appreciate levels of risk to the child, or riding roughshod over parental rights.

Issues over care proceedings were re-examined in an inter-departmental review published in 2006.[3] This had been stimulated by

---

[1] *Avoiding delay in Children Act Cases* (Lord Chancellor's Department, 1996)

[2] *Children Act Advisory Committee Annual Report 1991–92*

[3] *Review of Child Care Proceedings System in England and Wales* (Department for Constitutional Affairs and Department for Children, Schools and Families, 2006)

the work on legal aid reforms arising from Lord Carter's recommendations.[4] The review accepted a revised protocol, known as the Public Law Outline, launched nationally by the Minister for Family Justice, Bridget Prentice on 1 April 2008. This sought to streamline the process by reducing the number of stages from six to four, and requiring greater professional collaboration and better case preparation in identifying key issues prior to trial. Following the direction taken by Lord Woolf for the civil justice system,[5] this procedure front loads the process, and seeks to iron out issues of conflicting evidence before hearing. The statutory guidance for local authorities has also been updated, and will also require more work to be done before and at the time of issuing proceedings. The aims are laudable, but the main difficulty, according to the stakeholders consulted by the Ministry of Justice in July 2007, is that placing aspects of the work which have, over time, been taken up by the courts upon the local authority instead requires more and better staff resources within the authority. Furthermore, the changes suggested to the court process require more skilled intervention by the lawyers. Unfortunately, local authorities are short of funds and staff, and with the moves towards a market-based scheme for public funding which began in October 2007 taking effect, the courts may be severely handicapped by a lack of experienced care legal practitioners. The new scheme moves towards block funding to solicitors and fixed fees for barristers. Work will no longer be paid for according to the time taken. Those preparing these reforms appear to be unfamiliar with the way the work is carried out in practice.

II. Nadia's Case Conference

We start with a report of a case conference held in the morning prior to a court appearance in the afternoon. This was an early stage of a process that could result in a care or supervision order, although in this case the long-term plan was for the boy to return home. The client was a mother with an alcohol problem whose son was living with a relative under a residence order, but with weekly contact by the mother. The barrister, Nadia, described herself as doing the work of a solicitor at this meeting,

---

[4] Lord Carter of Coles, *Legal Aid: a market based approach to reform* (Department for Constitutional Affairs, 2006)

[5] Lord Woolf, *Access to Justice: Final Report on the Civil Justice System* (Lord Chancellor's Department, 1996).

because she was 'cheaper'. In fact she was not paid at all for this work, but the meeting was a necessary preliminary to the case in the afternoon. Her task was to 'keep everyone happy' and to 'move the case along'. The meeting between the social worker, senior social worker, guardian *ad litem*, child's solicitor, mother's barrister, and local authority solicitor was not minuted, but the child's solicitor took a note. There were concerns about not creating too wide a disparity between the living standard enjoyed by the child while he was with the relatives, and what could be expected on return home. The social worker made an off-the-cuff remark about how rehab is the best place to learn where to get drugs etc. This led to lengthy discussion about mental health review and testing the mother to see whether she was clean before contact visits. Nadia calmed all this down by suggesting that the remarks should be taken in the spirit they were intended and not made into a big issue. She said that the mother was doing her best, and needed to be selfish in order to concentrate on her rehab. The relatives rather than the social services department were seen as powerful in this situation, and the family had washed its hands of the mother.

Nadia pointed out that certain forms had not been used correctly, and the social workers claimed this was due to lack of funds and of staffing The barrister said that her role was to filter interactions, which meant interpreting things to the client and making things realistic, avoiding over-high expectations. The social services department urgently wanted to get the case off its books, but legally and procedurally was not in a position to do so. The barrister focused on practical aspects of time and place, adding that there was a need to think outside of the box and not to demonise this woman. Social services were reluctant to release documents about the suitability of the placement, but the barrister insisted that they could not go to court without doing so.

Nothing was finalised. Nadia spoke afterwards to the researcher about the department's wish to whitewash the mother, not following protocol, and push through a plan without checking. She expected that the hearing that afternoon would be adjourned for lack of papers.

III. Claudia and the Underweight Toddler

The barrister in this case, Claudia, had asked the researcher to accompany her to a case outside London, but at 8 pm the evening before called to say that she would be taking a different case in London instead. She was representing a local authority in the case of a two-year-old boy who was underweight and whose parents had learning difficulties. A supervision order had been made six months earlier, allowing the child to remain at home under tight conditions, including attendance by the parents at parenting classes. These conditions had not been met in full (the attendance had been intermittent) and the child had a cut to the head. The parents had meanwhile separated and reconciled, and another baby was on the way. The child had been moved under an interim care order to a foster carer, and this order was expiring on the day of the hearing. This was a relatively straightforward case. Claudia was representing the local authority, and the matters at issue concerned only the next steps in the process, and the parents did not object to the proposals. Nevertheless, the role of counsel in alerting the social workers to the parents' perspective, and setting the stage for a possible agreed outcome at the final stage became apparent.

Claudia met the social workers in the waiting area. They said they were pleased with the boy's progress, and praised the foster carer. They had visited the home to collect clothing, and though the mother had been helpful, they were concerned by the state of the place. They had concerns about possible domestic violence, and about the child's paternity. They were considering 'permanency planning' and wanted a full medical report. They said that the parents also wanted a report from an endocrinologist on the weight issue, so joint instructions were possible. Claudia said she could not see what a medical report would add: 'This isn't just a medical case', and she also asked 'why on earth is this being heard here?' The social workers agreed it should be heard locally, as the family lived in an outer London borough. Claudia said the location was due to lack of space and lack of magistrates. She then went to talk to the guardian *ad litem* and her solicitor. The researcher took the opportunity to talk to the social workers, who were critical of the bar 'asking stuff you don't need ... it's just a game'. But they were appreciative of the High Court. 'They look po faced but then cut to the chase . . . safe pair of hands ... but you have to wait for a date'.

Claudia returned and said: 'No one is pushing'. The parents wanted to put in evidence and ask for leave to consult with an organisation which specialised in supporting parents with learning difficulties to obtain an assessment. The social worker said wearily: 'We don't need it. How long would it take? What do they do?' Claudia said that she would get the details. She thought they should seek only one medical report, from a paediatrician who would advise whether an endocrinologist would be helpful. Claudia said that if she had been representing the parents, she would ask for another assessment, which should be specialist, and she would be taking a longer view as there was the new baby to consider. This can be seen as an attempt to encourage the social workers to see the matter from both sides, and prepare them for a possible response by the parents should they seek to reach agreement. But the social worker was not persuaded: 'We went through all this last year. We tried to bolster their parenting, they can't do it ... it would be just protracting proceedings'. Claudia then said that the guardian wanted a paediatric assessment, as he was worried about the injury, and 'it may be a different case from what we imagine ... not just failure to thrive. We need health visitor evidence, what she said and saw'.

The parents arrive, arguing with their barrister, who calms them down. Claudia starts drafting Proposed Directions about a paediatric assessment, and a request for health visitor statements. She says that the mother may have misinterpreted the feeding advice. She mutters: 'I wish I had standard directions on a laptop and could press a button'. But she is pleased that nothing is being contested at the moment. She gives her draft to the social workers to check, adding that she has been asked by the parents' counsel to say that they would like another session of contact each week. The social worker replies: 'We think Monday, Wednesday and Friday is enough, or they'll get the wrong idea'. Claudia says 'ok', and goes back to the opposing counsel and the guardian. The usher calls everyone in at 1.30. The district judge asks to be told who everyone is, says he has read the note, but does not greet the parents. Claudia opens, saying that the interim care order expires today, directions have been agreed and also interim threshold reasons. The district judge remarks that the interim order is removed, but that he cannot accept the threshold agreement as it does not deal with the welfare check-list. Claudia replies that the list was accepted at the local court earlier, and that there were serious concerns. Counsel for the parents says her clients were not given appropriate feeding instructions, and asks about the timetabling. Claudia replies that the next stage is the Case Management Conference, and the district judge asks when it would be. Claudia says that there is no set date, and also there is confusion about the location. The local authority would prefer the local court, and also the mother is pregnant. The judge says he has no strong feelings, but what if the case were to be sent back to his court? The mother's barrister says she would prefer continuity, but the baby is due in three months time. The judge suggests a compromise, with the Case Management Conference in his court, but mother need not attend and then the case could go back to the local court for the final hearing. All parties agree, dates are set, and the court rises. The judge gives the guardian responsibility for finding all the necessary papers, including those from the first hearing, and agreeing the appropriate bundle.

IV. Isobel's Directions Hearing

In the next case, the barrister, Isobel, was from London, and the case was being heard out of London. She was representing the father of a one-year-old child at a directions hearing regarding a late application by the child's grandfather to care for the child together with the father's step-mother. The child was subject to an interim care order, but had been recently on holiday with the parents, giving rise to concerns about possible abduction. Apparently the father was a well-known local character, with lots of charm, but unreliable. He was unlikely to turn up. The social services department was currently assessing the applicants. They had been willing to consider this arrangement until yesterday evening when some unpleasant information was volunteered to them by the father's mother about the grandfather's behaviour in the past. The status of this evidence was complicated by the fact that the informant was in a local mental hospital. The local authority was also thought to be arranging an independent social work assessment of the father, as he had fallen out with local social workers. But, according to the solicitor, this had 'fallen by the wayside'. Isobel could not understand why this assessment had not taken place. The solicitor said that the matter had got muddled up with the planning for the father's other two children by another mother who were also involved in proceedings and had recently been freed for adoption. The mother had not contested those proceedings but there had been some question about whether the father was putting himself forward as carer for them, but apparently he was not. He had failed to attend his anger management course, but had called in to say that he had contact today with the child, and so could not attend court. Isobel said that she was the fourth person in her chambers to be involved in this case, and only received the papers late last night The solicitor comforted her with the news that at least she has a good judge, 'a specialist ... with medical knowledge ... she won't let you pussyfoot around ... it's black and white with her'. He remarked that he always made an attendance note, 'so if a different barrister comes we don't have to rely on the client or the other side'.

The guardian's solicitor and local authority barrister arrive. Isobel wants the case to be put on later in the hope of getting the father to attend, but the usher says this is impossible. The judge has a full list. A rather aggressive barrister representing the grandfather arrives. Isobel directs her to the guardian and her solicitor. Isobel has had a chat with the local authority barrister, but they fail to agree anything. The local authority position is that they cannot make any decision about the grandfather without further checks, and their response to the father's request for an independent social work assessment of him is unrepeatable. Isobel says she is glad it's not really her case! All the lawyers meet, and decide that the final hearing should not take more than four days, not the seven originally set down. Isobel goes through the history. The father has a poor relationship with his parents; a sister died tragically; there is a history of drug use some years ago, and convictions for assault. A second cousin had appeared and made enquiries about the baby, but this came to nothing. The local authority barrister is friendly and warm, and wishes Isobel luck … 'head down!' No one has seen the mother. She didn't show up for the final care order or freeing for adoption. At 10.40 the local authority barrister hands over handwritten directions, and Isobel agrees a draft. At 10.45 everyone is called into court. There are four barristers: for the local authority, the mother, the father, and the grandfather. Also there are the grandfather, the social worker and the solicitors for the local authority and the mother. The judge does not greet the grandfather. She says that the timetabling is sensible and that if anything arises from the disclosure requiring directions, then to come back immediately. Otherwise the matter can proceed to final hearing.

This was an event where there was no dispute about the need for intervention, and the local authority was close to finalising a proposal for care. No great disputes seemed outstanding prior to final hearing. All that seemed left to do was completion of checks on the potential carers. Whether it was necessary for such a phalanx of lawyers to collect together in the court in these circumstances might be questioned, but despite the late arrival of damaging information about the potential carers the legal representatives were able to agree a reduction on the length of the final hearing.

V. Sarah and the Disturbed Client

In this case a local authority had stopped contact between a mother, who had a personality disorder, and her five-year-old daughter as the final hearing in a child protection case approached. Sarah was representing the mother in her application for contact to be reinstated. Sarah met her client outside this Family Proceedings Court in the Midlands half an hour before the time set for the hearing. The client was very anxious, but Sarah managed to find a room, and began with soothing chat about her new scarf, and 'a rainforest of paper'. She then moved to her queries: 'I need to ask two things … the report, a yellow thing, you have it here'. She checked that the client had seen the care plan, which had been drawn up on the last day they were in court, and that the Mental Health Crisis team were in daily contact with her, bringing medication. She asked her what term she was comfortable with to describe her mental condition. The client was content for Sarah to refer to a 'personality disorder', but added: 'To be honest, I have a schizophrenic personality. Sometimes I get feelings of anger; sometimes I just laugh'.

Sarah then addressed the question of giving evidence at the final hearing. She warned that it could be acutely distressing 'if you get examined in a hard way. 95 per cent of people find it distressing'. She added:

> I don't want the court to make a finding that would go against you. If the barrister said you threw a glass of water, you might want to defend yourself and the court might say you were defensive. I have a responsibility to you to make sure that we have thought this through. The legal position is that parents can be compelled to give evidence, but if there is a mental health history we can agree not to. Rules of evidence say they should hear from both sides, but we can hear a case by submissions only, which means that only the barristers speak. The court would hear less evidence and I couldn't challenge what the local authority says. I've spoken to (the solicitor) and I will try to get the local authority to agree for you not to give evidence.

The mother was worried lest she be thought weak. She said: 'I *can* speak if I have to', adding: 'It's their job to rattle you. Do you ever do that?' Sarah replied:

> Sometimes I have to ask hard questions, but I don't set out to rattle people. You may find hearing what the local authority says makes you calm or you may get angry. So let's check later. The other thing I wanted to ask you, on reading the paperwork it seems to me one of the difficulties over contact is a personality clash between you and the social worker and the supervisor. They are going to say it's entirely caused by your mental health. I want to say it's a clash of personality. It's stressful for you; they should have found you another worker. Are you agreeable to me putting this? When you're deciding how to run a case I sit in chambers and think this, but it's important you agree. I'm going to say they haven't made enough effort to support you. For example, they have trouble with you making notes at contact. The previous worker

didn't have a problem about this, she said you were doing it to assist you and it did help and you handled contact well. They say you looked angry. You say, 'just assertive'. It's very subjective.

The mother went out for a cigarette. Sarah commented to the researcher that she did not expect to win, as last week the mental health team were considering sectioning the mother. Sarah then met the guardian *ad litem* in the corridor. His report had come in that morning and supported contact until adoption, but did not restrict the search for adopters to open adoption, which would make it possible for contact to continue after adoption. The guardian stressed that there was no treatment for the mother's condition. He was sympathetic to Sarah's request not to call the mother to give evidence, but said: 'I don't want to leap ahead. It's got to be in context'. This was one of the key phrases used by professionals signalling disagreement without being confrontational. Sarah then went to the room where the local authority group were conferring, but they wanted more time before talking to her. There were at least six of them. Sarah told the researcher that a district judge once said to her that the local authorities and the guardians were like battleships, while representing the parents is like rowing a boat!

Sarah met counsel for the local authority in the corridor, and was surprised to find that he was from her chambers. They negotiated about the terms of contact, discussed whether the mother should arrive 15 or 30 minutes early to allow the social workers to assess whether she was in a good enough state for the visit to take place, and considered whether there might different workers. Sarah suggested that it might help the local authority at the final hearing if they could be seen to have been helpful. 'Elegant advocacy Mrs X' was counsel's sceptical response. Sarah said to the researcher in an audible aside: 'If he wasn't from my chambers I'd kick him!' This tension-reducing badinage is common, counsel for the other side being the friendliest face the barrister will see all day. At 10.10 the usher approached and asked how long they would be. Sarah replied that they might reach an agreed position on 'threshold', that is, the reasons why the local authority sought a care order. Sarah asked what the local authority would do if there was no agreement, and her opposite number replied that they had allocated three days for argument about the threshold, and could come back for a day for disposal (agreeing the care plan). Sarah had not yet seen the threshold document, but said that, as her client accepted her diagnosis, the contest would be about disposal.

The case is then called in. There are three magistrates, Sarah, and the usher. Sarah and the local authority's barrister ask for a little more time as they may reach agreement. The bench grants 30 minutes for Sarah to take the mother through the threshold document. Outside the courtroom, they discover that they have lost their room to others, and have to talk in the busy corridor, shared with a court hearing criminal cases. Sarah shows her client the document. She says she thinks it is reasonable about the contact visits. Sarah says: 'Sometimes it's like jumping through hoops to get the result you want. You have to be particularly courteous and put on a good front. It's worth it'. 'Sucking up', remarks the client: 'I just need that hug'. But she is delighted that she will be able to see her daughter next week. Sarah then goes to find counsel for the local authority, who has remained in the courtroom. He has persuaded the local authority to find another worker to support the contact visits. Sarah explains that local authority experience of mental health problems is varied. In this case the contact supervisors are Family Assistants with NVQs in childcare, but they are not equipped to support this mother. Sarah is pleased that she has the client's reaction to the threshold document. Usually it gets hammered out by lawyers, but with this time available they can try to get an agreed document so that they don't have to spend three days in court thrashing it out with witnesses.

After going through the document with her client, Sarah goes back to counsel for the local authority to say that the client disagrees with only one allegation in it: that she had left the child unattended in the doctor's surgery and that the child was brought home by police. The clerk calls everyone in to court. Sarah reports that the contact application is adjourned, that contact is established, that the threshold is being agreed, but that she is taking instructions on one amendment. The opposing barrister asks for directions, but the magistrates say that he does not need them. The barrister responds that, on reflection, he agrees. No order is needed for contact as the mother has agreed the conditions. Sarah asks for more time to agree the threshold and was granted 45 minutes, to return by 1 pm. Sarah now finds a room. She goes through her client's diary, noting the date and time of the appointment with her consultant at which she knows the child was present, so confirming her account that she only left the child in the doctor's surgery for a few minutes, and that the child was not taken home by the police. The client becomes distressed and begins to scream and shout. Sarah talks soothingly about swimming and yoga. The mother calms down. Sarah now goes to ask counsel for the local authority for the social work record for the day in question. This cannot be traced. The local authority then agrees the mother's account of this incident. All matters are now agreed, except disposal. Contact is to continue until the final hearing. Sarah says to the client that this will be hard. But the mother agrees that she can't look after her daughter. 'I can't do it. It's too hard. I can't cope. But she'd love me so much when she's older'. Sarah suggests that they meet for a chat before that hearing.

This barrister's skill and determination in hammering out an agreement with the local authority spared the client a very unpleasant three days in court disputing the threshold, as well as achieving agreement on contact up to the final hearing. The skills are essentially the same as those employed in financial cases: rapid mastery of detail, checking and re-checking the facts, people management, persuading the client to move to a position which is within the ambit of any potential adjudication, negotiating with the other parties and persuading the court to allow time for negotiation. Success was possible because the client had accepted that she could not cope with caring for her child.

VI. Peter and the Family of Five Children

This was a pre-trial review, and the barrister, Peter, was representing the mother. Peter and the researcher arrived at 9 am at the modern, quiet, court outside London. There were plenty of conference rooms. Peter explained that his client had been abused as a child, was in an abusive relationship and engaged in substance abuse. She accepted that this impaired her ability to care for her children. She had two children by another father. They were freed for adoption. This case concerned three younger children, and the local authority care plan envisaged adoption for the two youngest and long-term fostering for the oldest. Peter described his object as damage limitation. He aimed to make it possible that the oldest child could eventually come back. The 'threshold' grounds for intervention were 'light'; they related to missed medical appointments and poor school attendance. For the two youngest, he was seeking contact six times a year, but the local authority was offering once. The psychiatrist's report stated that the mother did not suffer from mental illness, only from the effects of a rough life, and that therapy was not appropriate. She said in her statement that she would love to have all three with her, but accepted that she had some way to go before she could meet their needs, and understood that the children couldn't wait. If they were not to be with her, she wanted them in placements where they were happy and could see each other. She promised that she would not undermine the placements if she had contact six times a year. The father had four other children. Three were adopted and one was living with a relative. The parents had met while on a residential assessment course for parenting their previous children. The father was a 'schedule 1' offender (that is, had committed certain sex offences). The psychiatric report found that the risk of him re-offending was moderate, but that the mother was unable to protect the children. The local authority was unsure whether to place the children together, and about the extent of contact to permit.

Peter's client was too upset to come to court, and had not given him any instructions. In fact, none of the parties were present, only their counsel and the solicitors. So Peter had the responsibility to look after the mother's interests in her absence. The local authority had noticed how 'light' the threshold grounds were and wanted 'stuff' back in. He was in difficulty because he could not take instructions. He was also stressed by the fact that the solicitor had repaginated the bundle at the last minute using an agency, and hoped he could muddle through. He did not want the local authority to think he was fighting anything or they would fight back. They were called in to court at 10 am. The judge said that they did not have much time, and that he was assuming this to be a pre-trial review but was not clear. He asked why the final hearing had been brought forward, and who would be hearing it, as it would not be him. The local authority representative explained that there were a large number of witnesses (over 20). The judge was unhappy about the late arrival of the synopsis faxed yesterday. He had not seen it. He observed that faxing 12 hours ahead was risky. He asked who was acting for the mother, and whether she was opposing the matter. Peter said 'no', but that she wanted more contact with the oldest child, who would probably go home eventually. He said that the mother was also hoping that the two youngest would stay with the present foster carer, but the local authority had said mother was not willing to consent to their adoption.

The father's barrister said that the father was opposed to adoption, and wanted long-term fostering. He confirmed that he was living with the mother. The judge asked whether this case would take five days. All counsel said: 'No, two or three'. The solicitor for the guardian *ad litem* said that the guardian was supportive of the care plan, but wanted detail about the placements before the final hearing. The solicitor said that there was a long wait for a panel hearing for freeing for adoption. The judge said: 'We are at the back of the queue. Why don't we jump it as this case has been going on for nearly three years … It is pretty miserable'. The judge raised the question whether the two youngest children could be placed together. The local authority was confident about finding a placement, but not together. The judge was not happy with this: 'They have been together throughout this miserable period. They will have derived some pleasure from each other's company. Are they now to be separated?' The local authority barrister said that they would see each other. The judge advised that he was only raising the questions that the adoption panel would raise, and that 'you will only get directions if the care plan is approved by me'. The local authority's barrister apologised, saying that the new legislation had created a backlog. The judge was not impressed. He pointed out that this is where opposition from the parents would arise. The father would challenge splitting up the two youngest, and the judge thought that there was something in that. He thought that maybe this is not an adoption case. The local authority maintained that their plan was realistic. The judge asked if the guardian could help with the expert evidence. But the guardian was not present. The judge then said that he had risk assessment charts he could not understand, a transcript of a conversation between two experts full of 'ums and ers', and asked why he couldn't have an agreed summary.

In planning for the final hearing the judge asked why there could not be written answers to some of the questions rather than days spent in the witness box, but the guardian's solicitor replied that father would need to be present as he challenged the care plan, even though he accepted that the children would not come home. The judge reminded them that the children were presenting with multiple difficulties, and looked for a date with the guardian. One was chosen. The social workers, who had been stuck on a train, now arrived. Peter explained that the mother was upset about the children leaving the foster carer, and he believed she was only asked about adoption at the last moment. Counsel for the local authority pointed out that one of the social workers would be on maternity leave on the chosen date, but that her manager could attend.

The judge tried to move things along, asking for a synopsis. The local authority said that they did not accept the mother's view on the threshold. The father was also seeking amendments, but he had only given instructions that morning. The local authority wanted a revised response to the threshold. The judge wanted that done in specific directions, and asked if there were any more issues. The guardian gave the list of experts attending. The judge asked for specific directions to be prepared by the bar to be ready by one minute to 11 on the first floor. He left. Counsel for the local authority started drafting, and at 10.45 the legal representatives were still discussing threshold. Peter explained to the researcher that this was not atypical chaos, as the hearing was in front of a recorder who was not familiar with the case. He told the guardian's solicitor that they would need a meeting the day before the hearing, and asked for the guardian's views on contact. The social worker was heard muttering: 'Five times ... what's the difference?' The local authority barrister returned with the draft and went to the first floor at 11 am to hand it in.

Peter returned to the conference room with the solicitor and spoke to the mother by mobile phone. He explained that he had been in front of the judge, who had not realised that the father was still fighting the case. He said that we wanted to deal with it realistically, and the judge said that he wouldn't be surprised if the oldest child ended up back home. Peter advised staying light on the threshold and not fighting or everything would be up for grabs. The father needed to do the same. He said:

> Don't lean on him, but get him to see his solicitor. We'll crack it ... that's our strategy. We want to get credit for avoiding hurdles in the future. And we've asked the judge to ask the local authority to give more detail about the care plans. I know you're unhappy about the boys not staying with the carer. Why not long-term fostering? In theory adoption is supposed to be the most stable arrangement, but why shouldn't the boys be together. (The father) needs to do some thinking. His statement needs to be in within a week. Sorry I couldn't sort it for you today, but it was not possible given that (the father) has a different view.

The mother expressed her gratitude. Peter tried to cheer her up by talking of a case where three children freed for adoption were back home three years later. He advised: 'Never say never'.

Although no final decisions were taken on this occasion, the exchanges would have alerted the local authority to points that would have been taken by the mother, and indeed the judge. The barrister's role meant that this mother could avoid the stress of being at court and feel confident that her position was being competently presented in its best light.

VII. James's Midnight Brief

James was acting for the mother in a pre-hearing review. He worked from London, and the case was in a County Court outside London. At 7 am, in the train, he showed the researcher an expert report of 40 pages which he had received by email at midnight, and which he was expected to understand and use by 10 am. The index to the file included matters on which to establish threshold, protocol documents, a social work chronology, applications and orders, Emergency Protection Orders, Justices' findings of facts and reasons (drafted by counsel), guardian appointment, interim supervision order, interim care order, evidence of parties, first social worker's statement, mother's statement, agreement between the mother and social services, statements by the father, the paternal grandmother, the health visitor, the social worker, interim care plans, second statements. Bundle 2 contained statements from the fostering social worker, evidence by experts and the guardian, assessments by a developmental psychologist, a child psychiatrist, an independent child psychiatrist, liver function tests, letters of instruction to experts, police evidence, and previous convictions of the parents (the mother and both fathers). There were records from social services, the general practitioner and the health visitor records.

The mother was married to Father 1. She was in her 30s, and had borne 10 children. She abused alcohol, and had failed to care properly for the children. A baby had died in infancy. Father 2 had parental responsibility over his two children with the mother, but there are issues about violent behaviour by both fathers. The eldest three were with her own mother, and not involved in these proceedings. The next oldest child, a teenage boy, lived with his mother. The next two girls were with a foster carer. The three little ones were with another foster carer but the paternal grandparents were being assessed as possible carers.

James said that the case would be a tough. There were children with differing needs, two or three legal representatives, and the case had transferred to the County Court because of its complexity. His view was that the local authority was just managing crises, not helping the parents to learn or manage the house. James was the fifth counsel to represent the family in four months. On arrival at the court, James found a room, and met counsel for Father 1. James wanted extra time for drug and alcohol test results. Counsel for the local authority asked if there was anything in the psychologist's report about an inappropriate relationship between father and son. James said there wasn't, although the report stated that work was needed on the relationship. The local authority solicitor suggested removing the hospital records from the evidence but James was more cautious, saying that he did not want to get to day seven and find that they were crucial. He said that he understood that there was a plan to remove the three youngest children to the grandparents that week. He says that his client opposed this, and wanted that to wait until the final hearing, to minimise the possible number of changes for the children. He pointed out that the current care plan did not include this move. He reminded everyone that the guardian was leaving the case and had made an application to be discharged from it. He wanted to go through the witnesses. There were seven for the local authority (the social worker, the health visitor, the social work manager, the guardian, and three experts), then the mother, the fathers, and the grandparents. The local authority barrister asked whether there would be another review. Why should the case not be on today? James replied that he had only just received the psychologist's report. Counsel for the local authority mentioned the liver test report and the guardian's report, which were still to come.

James said he had no instructions about the detail. The local authority barrister remarked that it shouldn't take 8–9 days as listed. As he saw it, the three youngest go to their paternal grandparents, the two older ones go into long-term foster care, and the oldest boy stays where he is with mum. Counsel for the grandparents asked what kind of order would be made to the grandparents. Could it be special guardianship? Could there be staying contact this weekend? James said he would agree if the judge requested that and the local authority barrister said the authority would proceed accordingly. The usher brought in the barrister for Father 2, who thought the hearing was next week.

There was some confusion between James and the local authority over whether this hearing was in fact the pre-hearing review. The authority argued that the only thing that could be contested was making a further interim care order, and that could be done by submissions. James replied that he could seek an interim care order with an undertaking not to remove the children from the foster carer. The local authority barrister retorted: 'No court would give you an interim care order. Let's be realistic'. James: 'I don't write the law ... if the court is not satisfied with the care plan, then (it might) ... we *are* being realistic'. The other conceded that the mother had the right to put her case.

The mother arrives happy. James says to her: 'I can make representations to the judge; he has limited powers. He can make an interim care order or not make one. It's unlikely that he will make one because then you'd be the only one with parental responsibility and he wouldn't be happy for (the children) to come back to you. The only basis would be if you promised not to seek their return. Have I got that right?'

She agrees: 'I'm contesting because it's only two months to the final hearing and they've had enough upheaval. They're settled where they are'. So she wants them to stay with the foster carers, and not go to the grandparents. James checks where the grandparents live, and who would have to change school and so on. James says that he can't make easy promises. 'The Judge may ask us to come back. I think it's unlikely the judge will let the children move today. Are you saying the grandparents are bad people?' Mum replies: 'No, but if they win it's another upheaval. I've already got S (one of the older girls) running to me out of school twice. I've to get her back to the foster carers. I'm told to call the police to take her back. How can I do that? This move is upsetting the older ones as well. Why do they have to stay in foster care and the younger ones get family?'

James replies that he read the report last night, all 80 pages. He says: 'I want you to go through it. I'm afraid it's not very encouraging for you. Basically it says really none of the children, including P (the oldest boy), should be living with you'. 'If they try to move P he'll kick off,' the mother interjects. James agrees: 'He'll vote with his feet. But it raises concerns. There is a lot about his emotional difficulties before the young ones moved. It's hard for the expert to say what is the cause. We need to see what social services and the guardian make of it'. 'I know what that'll be', the mother replies grimly. 'You're not in an easy position here', says James: 'You need to prepare yourself for the worst. As I said, it's my job to get the best result for you, but I have to give you realistic advice'.

The mother begins to cry. James gives her a crumpled tissue from his pocket. He says: 'I want you to talk to A (the solicitor) about this. She's the Rolls Royce of care proceedings. If my children were in this position I'd want to talk to her. Everything that could be done has been done here, but I don't want you to have illusions. From a lawyer's point of view the judges tend to follow the experts. It will be difficult to challenge the report. It's very thorough and fair to you. It's our job to look for bias, but the only bias here is in favour of the children. You may not agree. Any questions?' Mum mutters: 'What do you get for murder?' 'Whose?' 'The social workers, the grandparents. I'm doing everything they told me to do and they're lying. I'm not even allowed to see my kids on my own'.

James: 'The options to consider are not easy. It is not a final decision now, but if you were to agree the various proposals about where the children should live, then your views would be taken more seriously, because you would be seen to have a realistic view of where the children should be. What can I say to you? If the children are to live away from you, the judge's concern is for them to be secure. If he thinks you don't agree with the arrangement and are undermining it, then he's less likely to be happy with unsupervised contact. I still don't know what the care plan is, or what the guardian will say. If over the next few weeks when you've had a chance to read these reports and talk to others, if you reach the view that it's not going to be possible to have your children living with you, there is no point in putting yourself through the agony of a contested hearing. Some clients have said to me they would go ahead to show their children they fought for them. I think it's short sighted. If you agree in court to plans, it can be recorded that you're doing it to do the best for your children. It will be recorded and you can talk to them when they're adult. Children grow up feeling safe and secure when adults can agree. If there is constant war between you, it's hard. What I'm saying isn't easy. I want you to go away and think about it. Talk to the solicitor and guardian.

> The mother says that she never sees the guardian. James says: 'You will before he prepares his report. You'll be preparing a final statement to say how you feel. Any thoughts?' The mother says: 'My kids need a different social worker, especially the older ones. S wrote a letter to the guardian about it'. James: 'That letter will be considered'. Mum: 'I'm worried about S. She's run twice this week'. James warns: 'There will be suspicion you put pressure on her to write that letter. I'm sure it's not the case. The point is, social workers like to think they're good at drawing children out, but they are strangers'.

At 10.45 the usher called them in to court. Present were the judge, the clerk, barrister for the local authority, solicitor for the guardian, the mother, the grandparents, solicitor for the children of Father 2, social work supervisor, social worker, the mother's solicitor's clerk, and Father 2. James tried to comfort the mother on the way in, saying the judge might ask them to go out and talk some more. The counsel for the local authority suggested to James that he might ask for 30 minutes on exactly what the care plan was. James said he would, but that it took hours to get back into court at lunchtime. The judge asked to be reminded of the facts. Counsel obliged:

> The three youngest ones are in foster care: first issue. Second issue: the older ones in foster care say they are unhappy. I have spoken to the guardian and experts and they have not said they want to go home. Third issue: P, the oldest boy, is not subject to a care order but is in the proceedings. Side issue: the guardian is moving. I need to resolve this, and take instructions and convey to other advocates. Also we want to resolve the issue of witnesses; 15 in total. I have asked if we can narrow this down on the historical material.

The judge asked if anyone else wanted to say anything. James: 'Is there a letter from S in the bundle?' The judge did not know. James: 'I'll make a copy available'. The judge closed by saying he would see them at 2 pm, and if that was difficult, another court would be available.

At 11 am James goes back to conference room. He can't do much until the local authority representatives come back. He gives the 'S' letter to the guardian and his lawyer in the canteen. On returning to the conference room, he asks the solicitor if S wrote it off her own bat. She had no information. When the client returns from the smoking room, he asks her about the letter. Mum says that S wrote it when she got her back to the foster carers. James asks: 'What did the foster carer say?' 'Nothing', replies the mother. James asks: 'Did the social worker mention it'. 'No'. James says to the solicitor: 'So we have it in the file?' The solicitor replies: 'I can't see it'. James says to the mother: 'Don't worry, it's safe, we've got it. I want the court to see a copy. The difficulty is we've nothing from M (the other child). They both spoke to the guardian, Dr B and the social worker, and didn't say they wanted to come home'. The mother says: 'They just asked me about it the weekend before'. James says: 'Her statement says she said her main wish was for the little ones to come home. We can read into that that she wants to come home. It's so obvious she doesn't say it'. Mum: 'She walked out of schoolroom saying she was coming home. She says things to try please everyone'.

James remarks: 'I take your point. Dr B says S appears to be advocating on mum's behalf for contact. But people worry about that because she's taking on an adult role … not being a little girl. We have to face it: there's not a lot of evidence for moving S and M, but we're waiting for other people to come back to us. I'm happy to spend the time talking to you generally. Otherwise I suggest you go for a coffee or a smoke'. The client replies: 'I'll get a coffee. If it goes against me can I appeal?' James answers: 'I'll explain two things. An appeal … it is possible but we can only do so if the judge has made an error in law or a clear mistake, not just if you disagree. Appeals are difficult to make. I have never succeeded in any appeal against a final hearing'. The mother is anxious: 'If I don't get them back next month does that mean they can't come back till they're 18?' James mixes reassurance with caution, and some advice: 'We can't assume the same decision for each child. I expect S and M will be in long-term foster care, the three young ones for adoption if the grandparents don't succeed. I think the grandparents are more likely than adoption, but there is a risk if it was felt they could not look after the three without being hassled by you'.

The client responds: 'They won't get hassle from me, but I'll want to see them as much as possible'. James: 'You'll have to talk to the solicitor about that, you'll have to be careful if you pressure about their coming back'. 'I won't do that', assures the mother. 'It would just mess their heads up'. James underscores the importance of the point, and offers an encouraging prospect: 'You've got it in one. But as S and M get older and express a wish to come back to you, their wishes will be taken more seriously than at the moment. Once a care order is made it lasts to 18 but it's always possible to come back and ask for it to be discharged. For the young ones, I don't know if the local authority will want a care or residence order or special guardianship. That wouldn't take away your parental responsibility. I don't know yet what the local authority will say. Sometimes things change later. But I want to make clear to you that it couldn't be by clever work by lawyers but by clear evidence that it would be better for the children to be with you. Our solicitor can explain it again if you need. I'm going to the canteen. Come up and talk to us but steer clear of the guardian and social workers. I want them to get on with their talking today'.

The client has one more question: 'I got told to keep friendly with their dad. He sees P. Now the social workers tell me not to have contact with him, him not to come to mine. I thought the children could go to the grandparents better if their dad and I are getting on'. James says he will investigate. Mum says: 'On Fridays we all have contact together. The six kids and me and dad. Now they say 'don't meet!' James says: 'I'll try and find out'.

At 12.45, in the canteen, counsel for the local authority came over and said that the plan to move the children is on hold. They did not want them there with their father. Dr B's report raised concerns about him. They thought that the grandparents would find it hard to prioritise the children over their son who was living with them. More work was needed. They thought that S and M should stay where they were. S's letter raised concerns. Speaking of the little ones to live with me sounded like an adult role. So using the letter seems to have backfired! James asked them to keep an open mind. There were times when they wanted to live with their mother. The opposing counsel said:

> P is not an issue. We may want a supervision order, but we don't want to make him do anything he doesn't want to do. Can we look at timetabling? The final care plans about the grandparents are two weeks late, and may not be able to be finished for the Final Hearing. But they look ok. If they're not ok we will be seeking to free for adoption so we can go ahead with that, knowing everyone will contest it.

James said: 'Do you have any problem with timetable change?' Counsel: 'I can't object'.

James went back to find his client. He told the researcher that he thought this was a good outcome in the short term, but it makes adoption more possible, so he was glad he said what he did earlier to her. But it now depended on the behaviour of the father and his parents, not his client. The mother came back at 1 pm.

James says: 'We have good news in the short term but the worrying thing is they are putting the grandparents plan on hold. There are some worries. We need to keep this discussion private. Social services don't want the children living there while dad is there'. Mum says: 'He just told me'. James replies: 'There is a lot of gossip. Keep it to yourself. It's because if the children are to be looked after by the grandparents it's to be as parent figures, not by their father with the grandparents there. There will be a planning meeting next week'. 'Will I be invited?' asks the mother. 'Maybe not', answers James. 'The more people at a meeting the more complicated it gets. They have thought about S's letter. There are a lot of things in it but they're worried she is taking a parenting role'. Mum asks: 'What is it with S? She's lovely with the under fives, she loves them. She'll say: "Can I change the baby's nappy?" and I say: "No, I'll do it", but she likes babies'. James says: 'One thing to watch … that S might want a baby at an early age'. 'I say don't make the mistakes I did' replies the mother. But James responds: 'Children often do repeat the mistakes of their parents'.

The mother goes on to speak of her youth. James says how difficult it is and tells the Gillick[6] story, then that he thinks it unlikely P will be sent elsewhere. He asks her to have a think about what would help him. Mum says: 'He keeps on about an apprenticeship'. 'It's important', James responds. The mother expands: 'He's off drugs. The threat of being kicked out got him off. He's eating better … got a friend, a girl. He wants to go to college'. James says: 'Do your best. Do encourage him to talk to a guardian'. The mother says: 'I say we need to be open'. James moves on: 'Can we go back to the young ones. If it's not the grandparents, it's adoption. If that happens you'll not have contact'. 'It's not that I don't want the grandparents to have them', she replies. 'If adoption is the choice, I'd rather have the grandparents'. James says: 'I understand. It's clear that the court is unlikely to approve any of the children going back to you. I don't want to raise false hopes, but it might be more sensible for you to argue for the grandparents. But I don't know if their father would move out'. The client: 'He might. His mum and dad would finance a place for him'.

James seizes the slight opening: 'That's good news. Social services won't let the children live there while he's there. When they work out their plan they will be interested in your attitude. If they feel you might

---

[6] This refers to the well-known legal case of *Gillick v West Norfolk and Wisbech Area Health Authority* [1986] AC 112 (HL).

undermine the placement … it's subtle things … gentle persuading'. The client says she won't do that but James warns: 'It's not a question of not doing it but being *seen* to not do it. The letter from S raised the question of how powerful your influence is over the children'. The mother responds: 'The letter wasn't my idea. I was trying to calm her down'. James says: 'If social services accept that … to sum up, I'm reassured by what has been said today. We won't have any arguments in court today'. He goes to check out the position regarding Father 1.

The researcher was left with the client, who told her life story. James returned to say that the local authority said that mum spent the night with the father. The mother denied this and said that they are friends and were with other friends. James said: 'We can't dictate your life. They just want to know what the position is and need to hear the same thing from you and the father'. The mother: 'Ok'.

They went into court at 2.40. The barrister for the local authority thanked the judge for the extra time, informed the court that the plans for a move were on hold, and that the hearing was to be adjourned. Instead, they would hold a planning meeting about the concerns. The grandparents would be asked to respond the next day and on Wednesday they would all come back to court for review. James asked if counsel for the local authority has checked with the court.

The judge was irritated, pointing out that would clash with the fifth day of a five-day trial he was doing. He asked whether the issue was whether the child should go to the grandparents. The local authority counsel raised the concerns about presence of their son (Father 1) in their house. The guardian said that the grandparents did not see their son as having any part in the neglect. They saw themselves as working with the father in caring for the children, but did not see themselves as primary carers. This needed to be clarified. The local authority counsel said: 'Other parties want to come back to court sooner than the date set for 8–9 days'. The judge asked why this could not be moved along. Counsel said:

> We were waiting for Dr B's report. In the meantime contact has increased with the grandparents, which led to the meeting yesterday to review contact. We wanted to keep the final hearing date and want to explain our plans as they develop. The worst of all worlds would be if they want to be parties. Should they be joined now?

The barrister raised other issues: the mother's unhappiness regarding the position of S and M, and P (the oldest boy). The judge asked why was he not a party. The local authority had made an application for him but he was not the subject of any order. Directions needed to be re-timetabled. Counsel apologised: 'It is just an half an hour review, to tell the other parties the local authority's position'. The judge replied that if they were just giving information, a paragraph to others would be a helpful start, but was it necessary to come back? It was agreed that the local authority would file a position statement.

> James and the mother are content with the plan concerning guardians. The judge remarks that if the local authority thinks the grandparents won't do it, it isn't an option. James clarifies: 'The mother and father are not in a sexual relationship, but just friendly, and see this as helpful for the children'. The barrister for Father 1 says he has now seen the notes of yesterday's meeting. The father and the grandparents were not aware of the U-turn. Nowhere is there an understanding that the father should move out. Dr B says dad has potential as a parent. What caused the change? The judge asks about Dr B's report. The barrister says that the social work assessment of the father was positive. 'The local authority needs to nail their colours to the mast'.
>
> The judge remarks that he doesn't think that they need to gather together at great expense. A letter would do. He can't list a case of this magnitude at the drop of a hat. They are running out of time now. He asks whether there are other hearings before the final hearing. The barrister for the children (an older man) points out, with trepidation, that the guardian is leaving, and if they needed to they would have to postpone. The three youngest children were a particular problem. The guardian is concerned that the local authority could have changed their minds. The judge points out that time taken now may save time later. The barrister for the children observes that by everybody getting together before today, a lot of discussion has taken place, and progress has been made. The local authority recognises that the grandparents are perhaps not the right people. This is a difficult case. The older children are very fond of the young ones: sibling contact is very important. The guardian says this may be a vital feature of this case. The threshold is not difficult but resolution is. Half an hour's directions would be enough to enable a full hearing to go ahead.

They proceeded to talk about dates. The judge remarked that joining the grandparents was a discrete issue, and the barrister for the children wondered whether an order could be agreed administratively. The judge hoped that the local authority would explain their plans to the grandparents, because if they were going ahead with them then there was no need to join them as parties. He said he was inclined to say that the authority should explain and the grandparents should take advice. He added that they also needed a response from the parents on threshold and an indication of witness requirements. The barrister for the children said he could not identify his witnesses yet, and sought a meeting with Dr B.

The mother sat crying quietly throughout.

On returning to the conference room, James explained to his client: 'We're content with this. The grandparents will have an opportunity to become parties if social services say 'no' to them. The judge stressed sibling contact'. He added:

> You need to go away and think carefully about what position to take. I know you hoped the children would come back to you. I think if you can move on and be realistic, *not* reject your kids, but get on with things and have a decent relationship with them now … things look bleak now but if all six children can be secure and relaxed it will make it much easier for you to have a good relationship with them.

The mother asked: 'If the grandparents get the children, will they be able to take them out of the country?' James replied: 'If they have a residence order, yes for 28 days; if a care order, they will need permission of the local authority. What's your concern?' The mother: 'Will I lose parental responsibility?' James:

> No, you share it unless they are adopted. If a care order is made the local authority can overrule you. If it is a residence order, practical day-to-day decisions are made by the carer but you do not lose parental responsibility, just the right to say 'no', and you can go to the court about a prohibited steps order. Any other questions?

The mother had one: 'What's this threshold?' James explained:

> To have a care order, social services have to prove the threshold criteria and that an order is in the best interests of the children. Threshold means that at the time the children are suffering significant harm or were at risk of significant harm as a result of their care. To be honest with you they won't have any difficulty showing that. There's a long history of involvement. The sooner you accept these problems and move on … I'll report back to the solicitor.

At this point James left and returned to London, 12 hours after leaving that morning.

This account illustrates the difficulty of bringing together all the disparate elements of a highly complex, disrupted family into a state in which significant points of dispute can be resolved. It conjures the image of lining up restless horses at the start of the Grand National.

Here the mother ideally wanted the three youngest children back, and also to keep her son with her, but the local authority considered this unrealistic and was exploring alternatives. One was that the younger children should live with their grandparents, but that was complicated by the discovery that their father was living there as well. The court provided a focus for deciding what steps needed to be taken to prepare for an adjudicated resolution while respecting the interests of everyone concerned. Without her counsel, the mother would have been quite lost. Throughout, the barrister's role cannot be seen as anything other than supportive of the interests of his client while continuing to focus constructively on the interests of the children.

Epilogue

W E BELIEVE THAT the previous chapters will have conveyed a useful picture of what happens in family courts, and the part which barristers play in the action. We will try to summarise what we think are the main messages which the information projects.

I. Case Management and the Court System

The image of a court as a place of adjudication is far too simple. There are many kinds of hearing, and many stages on the way to final adjudication. Long before that ultimate event, there is a series of directions hearings and pre-trial reviews, at which the extent to which the evidence upon which a final determination could be made is assessed, both by the disputants themselves and sometimes by the judge. The judge may need to set out a timetable for the stages to come. In ancillary relief this may be a first appointment, followed by a Financial Dispute Resolution session, followed by a final hearing. During this process, orders for further disclosure of financial information may be made. In contact cases it is common for there to be an initial hearing, where plans are discussed and perhaps a CAFCASS report requested which may take some weeks or months to prepare. There may be interim orders for contact, which could be reviewed at further hearings. The process is often a gradual one as arrangements are tried out and parties given time to settle into the routine and gain confidence in the plan. In care proceedings the procedure is governed by the Public Law Outline, which sets out a timetable and procedures within which the judge will manage the progress of the cases.

It is possible to argue that some of these procedures are over-elaborate. One barrister, who described himself as a 'maverick', charac-terised the public law system as a 'Rolls Royce system for people without

Rolls Royces'. 'People can be paid £750 for nodding their heads and achieving nothing'. Case 6.IV, which involved attendance at court by four barristers for a date to be fixed for a later hearing, perhaps illustrates this. We wonder whether co-ordination through a court administrator, using appropriate IT, might not be more efficient in some circumstances. But it is not our purpose to explore ways of improving the administration and procedures of the courts (important as those things are). Our purpose is to show how barristers steer clients through the procedures as they presently stand, and how they try to move the dispute towards resolution before reaching the final adjudicative stage.

II. Mentor and Guide

The barrister is both mentor and guide for the client. It is an immensely concentrated and skilled task. It frequently involves mastering the papers in a very short time. Often they arrive at the end of the day for a case the following morning, requiring late night working at little or no notice, and a journey to court early the following morning. In Case 6.VII a key document had arrived at midnight. In a big money divorce case there may over 30 lever arch files, which must be not only read but carried to court. One barrister said that she reckoned each lever arch file took an hour to read. In care cases, the files may be swollen by expert reports, a lengthy social work report and witness statements. Facts must be verified and gaps filled wherever possible. In reading the papers, the barrister must be prepared to anticipate the position of the other side. He or she must conduct a self-dialogue on the lines: 'If I argue x, they might respond with y, but if I say a they could well respond with b ... they are likely to put forward d and I will answer with e, but if they put forward f I have little come-back so may need to put forward g'. The moves resemble a game of chess. Occasionally, though rarely, legal research is required, and sometimes a colleague in chambers will be consulted on a difficult technical point, such as the possibility of requiring a witness from outside the jurisdiction to testify.

Once inside the court building, the barrister sometimes needs to talk to the listing office and to the ushers about the list for the day. Having looked at the papers, counsel may confer with the solicitor if there is time, or if not, speak with the client. If this is a privately-funded case there may be a meeting or conference with the solicitor and client in chambers, but in a legally aided ancillary relief case such meetings are more likely to happen ad hoc on the day of a hearing, either in the court corridor or in one of the small conference rooms which are located in the court building near to the courtrooms. When this is a first meeting with the client (the solicitor may be present and he will have met the client before) counsel must very quickly establish a relationship with the client. This involves small talk, careful presentation of self, finding common ground, and emanating calm authority and warm support. These are all hard enough in an elegant meeting room of a specialist chambers but even harder in the busy court corridor shared with people involved in civil and criminal proceedings and no coffee bar or smoking rooms.

Counsel must then check facts, and rehearse the questions which it is anticipated will come from the other side. This must be done without sounding as if he has changed sides and forfeiting the trust of the client. This tough questioning can be hard for a client to understand, coming from the person who he thinks is on his side. Counsel must test his client's evidence without appearing to do so. A special coded language has developed: 'Can we expand this point?' (you are not telling me everything); 'this will raise questions from the other side' (they won't believe this for a minute); 'how would you like me to deal with these questions?' (tell me the true story *now*); 'if they say *x*, may I say *y*?' (how are we going to play this sticky one?).

As soon as the barrister has gathered and checked as much information as possible he will want to speak to the other side, but must first check the client's instructions. He will try to set out what the key issues are, what he thinks the other side will say, what he thinks a judge might find reasonable or what might be unacceptable, and then make sure that what he proposes to put to the other side is acceptable to the client. This may take some careful negotiation, as a client may be unhappy with any changes of plan which have resulted from the latest information. This process closely resembles the one we observed in our study of solicitors, where the first set of negotiations is with the client before reaching a position to be put, on the client's instructions, to the other side. The barrister follows the same procedure but starts with the information provided by the solicitor, and works much faster on a more tightly focused set of issues.

When counsel has ascertained that his instructions are clear, it is time to approach the other side. At this point the barrister escapes from close confinement and a difficult question and answer session in a tiny conference room with an anxious client and meets one of his own kind. Both know the name of the game, play by the same rules, use the same terminology and share the stresses of the job. It is not surprising that, although in one sense this is the most tense moment of the day, counsel tend to relax as they greet each other, and enjoy a release from tension as they play out their clients' stories and demands. When two experienced counsel who respect each other's work meet, it is unlikely that there will be no room for manoeuvre. How much give and take there is, and whether it will be enough for the case to settle, is the question. If one barrister is inexperienced, or is having difficulty in getting clear or sensible reality-based instructions, it may be difficult. The most difficult situation is where the other side is not represented, and counsel has to negotiate directly with an individual who is anxious, upset, angry, emotional rather than rational, and does not understand the process and the parameters of what is possible. In these cases it seems that counsel effectively plays the role of a mediator with expertise in the law and legal process.

By this stage they are often up against the court timetable. As the time for which they are listed approaches, they will be asked by the court staff whether they are ready. The usual answer is no. They need another 10 minutes, 30 minutes, 45 minutes. If the usher cannot get agreement to this, they may go into court and ask the judge or magistrates. The decision as to whether more time is granted is a crucial one. It will depend on the nature of the list for the day, whether any case has been adjourned, postponed or withdrawn, or whether any emergency matters have arisen. But it will also be affected by whether the judge has read the papers sufficiently closely to decide that there is any chance of further agreement. And finally the judge will be influenced by his assessment of the counsel. If they are known as barristers who are skilled in getting their clients to 'yes', they are more likely to be given more time to do so.

Adjudication is a rare event. When a matter is to be 'tried', in the sense of playing out a contest in front of the judge, the task of counsel on both sides is much easier, in that they simply have to present their own case. They are not also second-guessing and working with the other side of the picture. They can stop begging the judge for time, stop trying to persuade a recalcitrant client to accept reality. In a money case the hard work is then done by the judge who must take a view and work out the figures. In a contact case, lack of agreement is rare. In care proceedings a contested final hearing is rare, but when it occurs it is extremely distressing for all parties. Nevertheless, counsel find standing up in court stressful. If this point is reached they have lost control. They are in the hands of a judge. If before a High Court or Circuit judge, they face the assessment of their peers. If they are in front of magistrates, they face the authority of individuals who know far less than they do about the law. Either way it is not a route of choice.

Finally, when a hearing is over, the barrister faces the debriefing session with the client. In legally aided cases this work is rarely paid for, even though it often happens at the end of the day when everyone is exhausted and stressed. But many barristers go to great lengths to make sure that the client has understood exactly what has been decided and what will happen next. In privately-funded cases at least the time will be remunerated, unless the brief fee is an agreed amount for the whole event. But there, too, unless things have gone very well, this is hard task. In family law it is unusual for either side to get all that they seek. Every client comes to court because they are reacting to something which is unacceptable to them. As Cretney has observed,[1] given the complexity and level of distress and anger which now accompany the relatively small number of matters which come before the courts, it is hard to see how the courts can produce satisfied customers in the sense of making people happy.[2] Every barrister tries to get this something for them so far as it is feasible to do so. Clients rarely understand and appreciate what has been done. The solicitor has often had to leave to return to the office, and only the counsel on the other side will have any understanding of what has been achieved. It is not surprising, though sometimes confusing for clients, that counsel stick together.

What has been achieved? A dispute has been managed, *pro tem*. The available information has been rigorously tested, and hopefully this injection of reality has led to a settlement, though agreement may be too strong a word. Where agreement has not been possible, and any aspect of the matter has reached adjudication, the decision taken should have been reached which places the interests of any children first. A sometimes bewildered client has had the goings-on explained, been comforted, been protected from hostility from antagonists, been prepared for disappointment in the outcome and, perhaps most important, had his or her viewpoint represented. Given that any case which reaches a barrister, other than those where counsel is being used only for advice or settlement in conference, is deeply conflicted and entrenched, or, in a public law setting, has set up the state bureaucracy against an often vulnerable individual, this is an impressive result.

---

[1] S Cretney, *Family Law in the Twentieth Century: A History* (Oxford, Oxford University Press, 2003) 774.

[2] See for example Liz Trinder's account of contact disputes in L Trinder and J Kellett, *The longer term consequences of in-court conciliation* (Ministry of Justice, 2007)

III. Image and Reality

The intransigence which some people demonstrate in family conflicts can often seem incomprehensible to outsiders. It is therefore easy to ascribe its causes to circumstances beyond the wounded emotions of the parties themselves. Lawyers are an obvious target. Unfortunately, the history of divorce law makes this plausible. The determination of society that people should not be able to obtain a divorce by mutual agreement[3] meant that until recently divorce would only be granted if at least it appeared that one, innocent, party was seeking it as a remedy against the other, guilty, party. This forced people to emphasise conflict, and of course lawyers used the law to further their clients' interests. But lawyers also found ways round the law to secure divorces for clients who actually agreed their divorce and its conditions, despite the attempts of the legal and administrative processes to prevent this.[4]

Although some traces of this fault-based origin remain in the present divorce law, since the mid-1970s the policy has completely reversed, and now encourages agreement between divorcing parties. But this policy can no more eliminate conflict than the old divorce law could prevent people agreeing to divorce. So, whereas in former times lawyers tried to achieve the goals of clients who wanted to agree about their divorce by casting them in the unwanted role of adversaries in a hostile process, now they try to lead clients who are angry and intent on obstruction towards agreement.

There is a serious danger that the image of the legal process, and the role of lawyers within it, as being destructive and to be avoided as being a sign of shame and failure will lead to further erosion of the resources necessary to make it work effectively and humanely. There will always be cases where the intensity of the dispute, the complexity or opacity of the claims and counterclaims, or the significance of the outcome (such as removal of children) are such that agreement outside the court system will not occur. There must be a place where the wounds of victims of these conflicts can be, if not completely healed, at least dressed so they can resume their lives. This is not done well in under-resourced premises, served by antiquated IT systems and overstretched staff,

---

[3] On which, see Cretney, above n 1, at 243.
[4] See Cretney, above n 1, at 259, for an example, and, generally, J Eekelaar, 'A Jurisdiction in Search of a Mission: Family Proceedings in England and Wales' (1994) 57 *Modern Law Review* 839.

located in inadequate premises and where the victims' guides and mentors (the barristers) are frustrated and de-motivated.

We hope that we have shown that society should value their contribution more.

Index